Walk Around

D1555920

AH-1 Cobra

By Wayne Mutza

Color by Don Greer and Richard S. Dann

Illustrated by John Lowe and Richard Hudson

Walk Around Number 29

squadron/signal publications

Introduction

Bell's **AH-1 Cobra** attack helicopter needs little introduction. It fulfilled the US Army's requirement for a weapons platform to protect troop transport helicopters during the Vietnam War, since the Bell **UH-1C Iroquois 'Huey'** gunship was unable to escort the faster transport helicopters. Bell Helicopter wisely anticipated this need and began its own research and development of a faster, more powerful, and more heavily armed gunship in 1965. The sleek and lethal **AH-1G** Cobra satisfied the Army's urgent requirement for a pure gunship in the intensifying war. Shortly after its arrival in Vietnam during mid-1967, the Cobra quickly earned the respect of its fixed-wing contemporaries. Its combat roles were expanded to include anti-armor missions using the Hughes BGM-71 TOW (Tube-launched, Optically-tracked, Wire-guided) anti-armor missile. This foreshadowed the conversion of half of the Army's Cobras to anti-armor platforms during the mid-1970s to counter the Warsaw Pact armor threat in Europe. The Army continually upgraded its Cobras – through the **AH-1Q**, **AH-1S** (in four sub-variants), and **AH-1F** models – before they were replaced in favor of McDonnell Douglas (now Boeing) **AH-64 Apaches** during the late 1980s.

The US Marine Corps (USMC) closely watched the Army's success with Cobras and operated a small number of AH-1Gs in Vietnam. The Marines then ordered a slightly larger and more heavily armed twin-engine version, the **AH-1J SeaCobra**, which entered service in 1969. The USMC prefers twin-engine helicopters for greater overwater safety. In 1976, powerplant improvements led to the **AH-1T**, which carried more than twice the AH-1J's payload. Further refinement of the 'Tango' resulted in the **AH-1W** (formerly **AH-1T+**) **SuperCobra** of 1986. The 'Whiskey' Cobra remains the only attack helicopter with dual anti-armor capability. It can use either the TOW or Rockwell AGM-114 Hellfire (HELicopter Launched FIRE and forget) missiles against armored vehicles. A major upgrade of the 'Whiskey' to meet expanding mission requirements will extend the Marine Cobra's service life until 2025. The new generation **AH-1Z** incorporates the latest technology to form a totally integrated weapons platform.

Since the Vietnam War, the battle-proven family of Cobra helicopters has served in many global trouble spots, a trend that will continue with the new 'Zulu' SuperCobra. This work presents the Cobra's lineage through successive models.

Acknowledgements

I am indebted to the following for their unflagging support of the preparation of this book: Bell Helicopter Textron, Inc.; Sean M. Borland; John Hairell; Renee Hatcher, US Navy Public Affairs; Butch Lottman; Lennart Lundh; Tom Maloney; SSGT David Roof USMC/Orion Decals, and Frank White.

(Front Cover) VooDo LADY is an AH-1G Cobra assigned to the 11th Armored Cavalry Regiment in Vietnam during 1969. Helicopters of US Army air cavalry units in Vietnam were identified by crossed sabers. The parent unit's insignia was usually painted on the Cobra's rotor pylon, also called the 'dog house.' This 'Snake' is armed with a 7.62mm Minigun and 40mm grenade launcher in a chin turret, with rocket launchers and a podded Minigun mounted on its wing stations.

ISBN 0-89747-438-4

If you have any photographs of aircraft, armor, soldiers or ships of any nation, particularly wartime snapshots, why not share them with us and help make Squadron/Signal's books all the more interesting and complete in the future. Any photograph sent to us will be copied and the original returned. The donor will be fully credited for any photos used. Please send them to:

Squadron/Signal Publications, Inc.
1115 Crowley Drive
Carrollton, TX 75011-5010

Если у вас есть фотографии самолётов, вооружения, солдат или кораблей любой страны, особенно, снимки времён войны, поделитесь с нами и помогите сделать новые книги издательства Эскадрон/Сигнал еще интереснее. Мы переснимем ваши фотографии и вернём оригиналы. Имена приславших снимки будут сопровождать все опубликованные фотографии. Пожалуйста, присылайте фотографии по адресу:

Squadron/Signal Publications, Inc.
1115 Crowley Drive
Carrollton, TX 75011-5010

軍用機、装甲車両、兵士、軍艦などの写真を所持しておられる方はいらっしゃいませんか？どの国のものでも結構です。作戦中に撮影されたものが特に良いのです。Squadron/Signal社の出版する刊行物において、このような写真は内容を一層充実し、興味深くすることができます。当方にお送り頂いた写真は、複写の後お返しいたします。出版物中に写真を使用した場合は、必ず提供者のお名前を明記させて頂きます。お写真は下記にご送付ください。

Squadron/Signal Publications, Inc.
1115 Crowley Drive
Carrollton, TX 75011-5010

(Previous Page) After initial tests, the first AH-1W 'Whiskey' Cobra (BuNo 161022) was painted in this striking black and gold scheme. An advanced version of the US Marine Corps AH-1T, the 'Whiskey' became operational with Marine squadrons in 1986. These units then boasted the most powerful and versatile attack helicopter in the world. (Bell)

(Back Cover) US Army AH-1F Cobra variants, armed with 20mm cannon, TOW missiles and rockets, were the scourge of Iraqi armor and fortifications during Operation DESERT STORM. This AH-1F (67-15883) began life as a Vietnam-era AH-1G and was converted to an AH-1S before upgrading to AH-1F standard. It didn't take long for Cobras painted with low infrared Sand (FS33717) for the desert war to acquire this weathered appearance.

Bell's original Model 209 (N209J, foreground) flies with the first two AH-1G prototypes (66-15246 and 66-15247). The Model 209 was Bell's answer to the US Army's search for a turbine engine-powered pure attack helicopter. It first flew on 7 September 1965 and was painted overall Olive Drab (FS34087) with both US Army and civilian markings. White checks on 66-15246's aft fuselage were used for camera tracking. (Bell)

Fitted with flight test equipment on its rotor mast and nose, this early AH-1G is armed with a 19-tube 2.75 inch (70MM) XM-200 rocket pod. An XM8 smoke grenade dispenser was attached to the XM-200's undersurface. Red rectangles were painted ahead of the windshield and below the pilot's canopy. Early Cobras displayed the last two digits of their constructor's number in red – here, 39 – on the rotor pylon. (Bell)

The fifth Cobra built (66-15249) displays the features familiar to early models, including nose landing lights, one turret-mounted 7.62MM Minigun and the tail rotor mounted on the port side of the tail fin. The aerodynamic 'surfboard' atop the rotor pylon prevented stalls behind the rotor mast and the disc above it simply covered the pylon opening. The slim profile and tandem seating is standard for all Cobras. (Bell)

Two AH-1Gs assigned to the 5th Aviation Detachment undergo a 100-hour inspection at Vung Tau, South Vietnam during 1970. Most major access panels are removed for the inspection. Crewmen service the lead helicopter's front cockpit, main rotor hub, engine, and tail rotor. Cobras were found to be extremely durable in Vietnam's tropical climate. (US Army)

The sixth production AH-1G (66-15250) is painted in this Gloss White (FS17875) and Insignia Red (FS11136) scheme for Arctic tests at Fort Richardson, Alaska in 1968. The only Cobras known to have worn the high visibility scheme are trainer aircraft and those assigned to Alaska-based units. (Bell)

SUZE Q III was a sharkmouthed AH-1G assigned to C Troop/16th Cavalry at Can Tho, South Vietnam during 1972. This Cobra is fitted with an extended exhaust nozzle, which redirected hot exhausts towards the main rotor wash to reduce the heat signature. The nozzle was developed to counter North Vietnam's *Strela 2* (SA-7 'Grail') shoulder-launched heat-seeking Surface-to-Air Missiles (SAMs). The access door for the nose turret ammunition bay is open. (Hugh Mills)

This early AH-1G is armed with a single 7.62MM General Electric (GE) XM-134 Minigun in the Emerson TAT-102A nose turret. The pod-encased 7.62MM XM-18 Minigun on the inboard stub wing was later replaced by either a 20MM GE XM-35 cannon or by a rocket pod. One seven-tube 2.75 inch XM-157 rocket pod is mounted on the outboard stub wing. (Ron Osborn)

The AH-1G's gunner/copilot sits in the front cockpit. The articulating turret sight occupies the center of the cockpit, while armchair controls for flying the aircraft are placed along both sides. The combination throttle and collective (pitch control) lever is mounted on the port side console, while the cyclic (directional control) grip is placed to starboard.

The collective/throttle lever is mounted beside the port wall of the pilot's aft cockpit. A trigger at the front of the cyclic grip fired the turret-mounted weapons only when fixed forward. The red offset switch on the grip's left side launches wing ordnance. AH-1G cockpits were painted Dark Gull Gray (FS36231) with Instrument Black (FS27038) panels.

The pilot's XM-73 reflector weapons sight is mounted atop the instrument panel shroud. Armament control and communications instruments were placed on the port instrument panel side, while flight control instruments were mounted to starboard. Tail rotor directional pedals are embossed with BELL to port and COBRA to starboard.

5

The Cobra pilot is positioned behind and slightly above the gunner/copilot's position and both are well shielded by boron carbide armor panels. The forward canopy opens to port, while the pilot's opens to starboard. Cockpit lights are attached to the right armor panel and the large-diameter tubing directs hot or cold air to the seats. The screened rectangular opening at the base of the rotor pylon is a transmission cooling intake. (Bell)

Pilot and gunner/copilot seats are of meshed material fitted over seat frames to allow air circulation. The upholstery is light green with an olive green trim. 'Armchair' flight controls and armrests are on each side of the forward seat to allow room for the floor-mounted sighting apparatus. Some AH-1G canopy latches are flush-mounted. (Bell)

The pilot's cockpit enclosure opens to starboard on this early AH-1G (66-15283) and all other Cobras. Light gray air ventilation ports are mounted at each lower end of the instrument panel. Cables for the emergency canopy removal system are attached to the canopy framework. Either crewman can detonate the explosive material to jettison the canopy from the aircraft in an emergency. (Bell)

Ground crewmen load linked 7.62MM ammunition for the turret machine gun into an AH-1G in May of 1970. The Cobra was assigned to C Troop, 1st Squadron/9th Cavalry Regiment, 1st Cavalry Division in Vietnam. The turret panel is removed to check the gun's feed mechanism after loading. The ammunition bay holds 4000 rounds for the nose turret weapon. (David Dzwigalski)

M28 Turret

Minigun and grenade launcher installation varied on AH-1Gs.

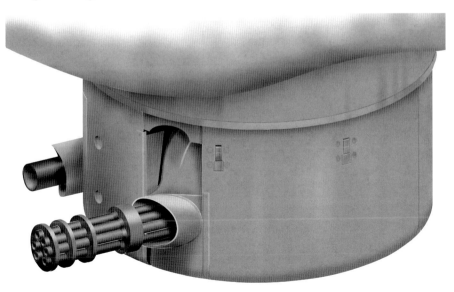

The Emerson M28 turret replaced the interim TAT-102A single-weapon turret on later AH-1Gs. The M28 contained one 7.62MM GE GAU-2AB/A 7.62MM Minigun and one 40MM Hughes M129 grenade launcher, or two of each weapon. The machine gun fired either 2000 or 4000 rounds per minute (RPM) in six-second bursts. The M129 was supplied with 231 rounds, which were fired at a rate of 450 RPM. Both weapons could be fired simultaneously. (C.M. Reed)

This AH-1G of D Troop, 229th Assault Helicopter Battalion, 1st Cavalry Division in Vietnam in 1969 is armed with a 19-tube XM-200 rocket pod and a 7.62MM XM-18 Minigun. The cable attached to the engine access door's interior surface is a fire-warning element. On rare occasions, Cobra pilots carried rescued aircrew on the opened turret ammunition bay door. A patched bullet hole is located on the lower fuselage. (George Sullivan)

The ordnance package commonly carried on the starboard stub wing of AH-1Gs in Vietnam comprised the seven-tube XM-158 and 19-tube XM-200 rocket launchers, called 'Hog' pods. The XM-200's leading edge has a notched ring for attaching breakaway fairings, which were seldom used. The port stub wing usually consisted of a similar arrangement or a rocket pod outboard and a Minigun inboard. (William P. White)

Spring-loaded, electrically fired igniter arms are fitted to the rear of all rocket pods, including this XM-158. The igniter arms are moved to the outside of the tubes for rocket loading. Electrical impulses sent by the firing buttons in the cockpit ignite the solid rocket motors, launching the rockets out of the tube. (William P. White)

2.75 Inch (70MM) Folding Fin Aircraft Rockets (FFARs)

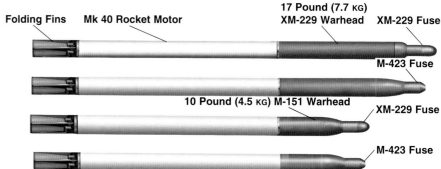

Folding Fins | Mk 40 Rocket Motor | 17 Pound (7.7 KG) XM-229 Warhead | XM-229 Fuse
M-423 Fuse
10 Pound (4.5 KG) M-151 Warhead | XM-229 Fuse
M-423 Fuse

FFAR Launchers

7-Tube XM-157 Launcher

7-Tube XM-158 Launcher

19-Tube XM-200 Launcher

Beginning in 1969, Army Cobras in Vietnam were given more firepower with the 20MM General Electric XM-195 six-barrel cannon. It was carried on a special mount on the port inboard wing station. The XM-195 was often used in conjunction with a 7.62MM XM-18 Minigun mounted on the starboard wing station. (US Army)

The XM-35 system included a streamlined fairing attached to the fuselage, which held 1000 rounds of ammunition for the 20MM XM-195 cannon. Raised panels below the port canopy side contained system wiring. The openings of 19-tube XM-200 rocket pods were often kept covered, since their tubes and electrical connections were sensitive to corrosion and dirt. (Terry Love)

A late production AH-1G prepares to take off on another mission over Vietnam. Doors for the nose avionics bay and turret ammunition bay are open for pre-flight inspection. A seven-tube XM-158 rocket launcher is mounted on the right outboard wing station with a 19-tube XM-200 pod inboard. (William P. White)

A late production AH-1G flies low over its base prior to departing for another escort mission over Vietnam. No weapon is mounted in the turret and an XM-200 rocket pod is fitted to the inboard left wing pylon. The nose art depicts the Road Runner cartoon character with a machine gun at his feet. Late production AH-1Gs had the tail rotor moved to the starboard fin side for improved yaw control. (William P. White)

An XM8 smoke grenade dispenser is attached to the seven-shot XM-157 rocket launcher of this AH-1G in 1967. Twelve smoke grenades are carried by the XM8 to provide a smoke screen for the Cobra. Rocket launchers have notched rings on both ends for attaching breakaway fairings. The engine air inlet is covered with a fine-screen material to prevent Foreign Object Damage (FOD) to the engine. The fuel filler cap is placed forward of the stub wing and the ground wire receptacle below the canopy frame. The panel immediately aft of the canopy provides access to the hydraulic reservoir. (Bell)

An XM-18 7.62mm Minigun and XM-200 rocket launcher occupy the port wing of this 9th Infantry Division AH-1G in Vietnam in 1967. The forward half of the Minigun's pod is removed. The 2.75-inch (70mm) rockets used either ten pound (4.5 kg) or 17 pound (7.7 kg) warheads and could be fired in pairs or ripple-fired at a rate of six per second from each launcher. Rockets were aimed using a Mk 18 sight in the cockpit. Either pilot could jettison rocket pods in an emergency. (US Army)

The 20mm XM-195 six-barrel cannon was basically similar in appearance to the 7.62mm XM-18 Minigun. The XM-195 featured an ejection chute under the breech mechanism to prevent empty shell casings from striking the tail rotor. (Charlie Palek)

A Fairchild Hiller employee holds up an XM8 smoke grenade dispenser, manufactured by this company. This dispenser was strapped beneath a rocket pod and held 12 smoke canisters, although only 11 canisters were fitted to this XM8. The smoke canisters were used for marking targets for other helicopters or for laying protective smoke screens. (Bell)

Unlike their Huey cousins, few Cobras flew in Vietnam in other than overall Olive Drab (FS34087) paint schemes. This exception, armed in a 'Heavy hog' configuration, has the markings of B Battery, 2nd Battalion, 20th Aerial Rocket Artillery, 1st Cavalry Division. Its single-weapon turret and extreme weathering suggest it may have originally been assigned to the Cobra New Equipment Training Team (NETT), which gave the Cobra its first taste of combat in 1967. NETT was known to have camouflaged at least two AH-1Gs in Tan (FS30219) and Dark Green (FS34079). (Bell)

Thirty-eight AH-1Gs were diverted from the US Army to the US Marine Corps in early 1969 for use in Vietnam, pending delivery of AH-1Js. Marine Cobra tactics were much the same as those used by the Army; however, the Marines added armed reconnaissance missions. This example (68-15046) is armed with a rocket pod and a Minigun on the port stub wing.

Marine AH-1Gs wore overall flat Field Green (FS34095), with International Orange (FS12197) training markings. The tailband and rotor tips are painted Orange Yellow (FS13538). (US Marine Corps)

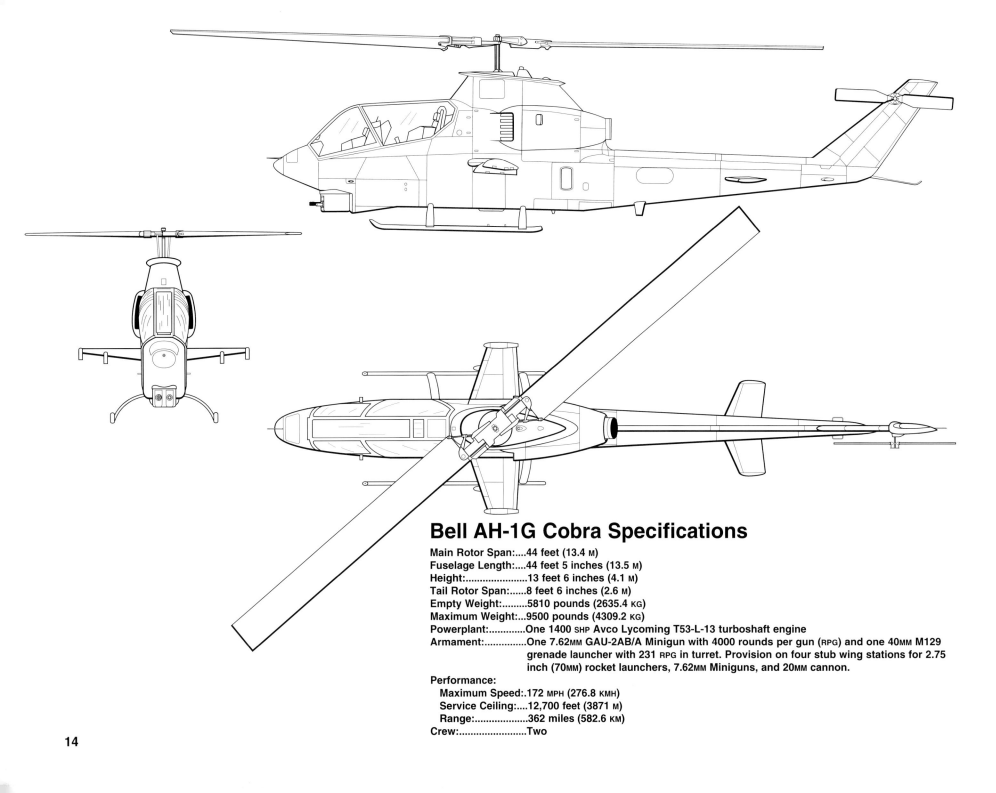

Bell AH-1G Cobra Specifications

Main Rotor Span:....44 feet (13.4 м)
Fuselage Length:....44 feet 5 inches (13.5 м)
Height:.....................13 feet 6 inches (4.1 м)
Tail Rotor Span:......8 feet 6 inches (2.6 м)
Empty Weight:.........5810 pounds (2635.4 кɢ)
Maximum Weight:...9500 pounds (4309.2 кɢ)
Powerplant:.............One 1400 sнᴘ Avco Lycoming T53-L-13 turboshaft engine
Armament:...............One 7.62мм GAU-2AB/A Minigun with 4000 rounds per gun (ʀᴘɢ) and one 40мм M129
                                  grenade launcher with 231 ʀᴘɢ in turret. Provision on four stub wing stations for 2.75
                                  inch (70мм) rocket launchers, 7.62мм Miniguns, and 20мм cannon.

Performance:
  Maximum Speed:.172 мᴘʜ (276.8 кмʜ)
  Service Ceiling:....12,700 feet (3871 м)
  Range:....................362 miles (582.6 км)
Crew:.........................Two

A small number of TH-1Gs were used for training, including this example assigned to the 9th Infantry Division at Fort Lewis, Washington State in 1972. These aircraft usually had dummy nose turrets and empty ammunition bays. Like front line Cobras, the TH-1G's tail rotor was repositioned to the starboard side of the tail fin. The nose avionics bay door, main rotor pylon, and aft engine enclosure are International Orange (FS12197). The forward fuselage code 49F is white; all other markings are black on the Olive Drab (FS34087) aircraft. (AAHS)

The AH-1G's 540-rotor system was pioneered on the Bell UH-1C Iroquois 'Huey' gunship. This semi-rigid 'door hinge' system was simple, required little maintenance, and enhanced the helicopter's performance. The 27-inch (68.6 CM) wide chord rotor blades allowed high speed maneuvering. The flush-mounted door on the rotor pylon ('doghouse') provided access to rotor components. (Bell)

All Cobra models use the same 42° gearbox incorporated into the tail rotor drive shaft. Two technicians service the drive shaft of a later AH-1F Cobra. The drive shaft is mounted along the upper edge of the aft fuselage and enclosed by 'tunnel' covers hinged to the side for access. (Butch Lottman)

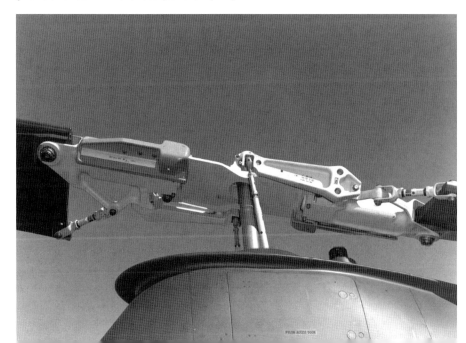

15

The AH-1Q resulted from mating the AH-1G with the Hughes BGM-71 TOW (Tube-launched, Optically-tracked, Wire-guided) missile system in 1973. This weapon – mounted in four-tube launchers under each stub wing – allowed the Cobra to successfully engage enemy armored vehicles, day or night. A turret-mounted Hughes M65 Telescopic Sight Unit (TSU) was mounted in the nose, enabling the copilot/gunner to aim the TOW at its target. The structure was strengthened to handle the 500 pound (226.8 KG) increased weight and the blast forces from the TOW's launch. The pitot tube was relocated from the nose to the rotor pylon. The AH-1Q retained the AH-1G's 1400 shaft horsepower (SHP) Avco Lycoming T-53-L-13 turboshaft engine. This Cobra (70-16055) was the first AH-1G converted to AH-1Q standard. (Bell)

Hughes BGM-71A TOW

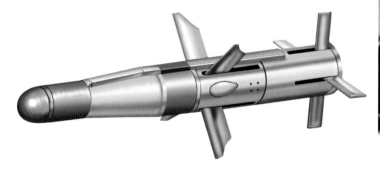

BGM-71A TOW Specifications

Length:....................................45.8 inches (116.3 CM)
Diameter:...............................6 inches (15.2 CM)
Weight:..................................41.5 pounds (18.8 KG)
Explosive Warhead Weight:.5.4 pounds (2.4 KG)
Range:....................................3000 M (9842.5 feet)
Maximum Velocity:................299 M (981 feet) per second

Two-Tube TOW Missile Launcher

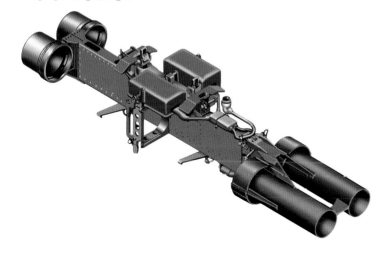

The gunner/copilot's position of the AH-1Q is dominated by the centrally mounted TOW sighting unit. The two columns of master caution lights are placed on the instrument panel's center section. The TOW control panel fills most of the starboard instrument panel. The orange-painted azimuth (horizontal bearing) indicator is mounted on the M65 TSU, ahead of the canopy. This indicator aided the gunner in tracking targets. (Bell)

This Cobra (70-16031) began as an AH-1G and was among the first to be converted to AH-1S standard. This version was TOW-equipped and brought up to ICAM (Improved Cobra Agility and Maneuverability) standards, which included the more powerful 1800 SHP T53-L-703 engine and structural strengthening. This variant comprised the Cobra fleet in Europe during the late 1970s. It is fitted with the original heat-dissipating exhaust extension. The 7.62MM ammunition bay and the transmission and tail rotor drive shaft panels are opened for servicing. (Dennis Goodwin)

The AH-1S retained the AH-1Q's M65 Telescopic Sight Unit (TSU) in a nose turret. The visual sight in the port side allowed the gunner to sight targets and aim weapons in all lighting conditions. The door on the TSU's starboard side covered a laser rangefinder, which was accurate to 10,000 M (32,808.4 feet). (C.M. Reed)

The 7.62MM GAU-2AB/A Minigun is fitted on the M28 turret's starboard side, while the 40MM M129 grenade launcher is located to port. The gunner/copilot traverses the turret through 230° of azimuth and elevates the weapons from +20° to -50°. The TSU turret is mounted above and in front of the M28 turret. (C.M. Reed)

The TSU and the turret weapons are removed from this Cobra and a shield is temporarily fitted to the TSU housing. A cockpit access step for the gunner/copilot protrudes from the fuselage. The landing light was relocated to the left skid when a Night Vision Goggle (NVG) light was installed in its original belly location. A light gray L is painted on the rotor pylon. (Author)

18

The AH-1S introduced a cable strike protection kit to the Cobra series helicopters. Rails attached to the canopy windshield frame guide the offending telephone or electrical power cable to the cutter at the base of the rotor pylon. Cables are the greatest danger to helicopters flying at low altitude and high speed. (Author)

The pilot's armored seat panel is larger than the one fitted to the gunner/copilot's seat. The smaller size gives the gunner/copilot just enough room for egress from the smaller canopy opening. Cobra crews wear armored 'flak jackets' for additional protection from enemy fire. Only one strut is necessary for opening the gunner/copilot's canopy. (Author)

Two struts support the pilot's canopy door at its extreme front and rear. The electrical grounding port is located immediately aft of the canopy. The single-point fuel filler cap is fitted aft of and below this port. The pilot's side armor panels provide a considerable amount of protection from enemy fire. (Author)

The AH-1S's cockpit interior – including the soundproofing materials on the aft cockpit bulkhead – is Flat Black (FS37038) to allow for optimal NVG use. Earlier Cobras had Dark Gull Gray (FS36231) as the primary cockpit color. The large air hose behind the pilot's seat leads to the Environmental Control Unit (ECU) compartment behind the bulkhead. (Author)

This AH-1S (68-15204) was assigned to the Massachusetts National Guard in 1991. One 2.75 inch (70MM) practice rocket protrudes from the inboard seven-tube M260 launcher. This M260 is a more versatile and lightweight replacement for the XM-157/158 launchers used on earlier Cobras. The AH-1S is overall Helo Drab (FS34031), which replaced Olive Drab (FS34087) on US Army Cobras after the Vietnam War. (Candid Aero Files)

Red protective panels cover the TSU lenses when the TOW system is not used. The gunner/copilot's canopy opens on the port side and the pilot's to starboard on all Cobras. Canopy doors are held open with slender gas-operated cylinders. These early model AH-1S helicopters carry seven-tube XM-158 rocket launchers inboard of the TOW launchers. (Bell)

A canvas tarpaulin covers nearly all of this AH-1S's canopy, protecting the canopy from scratches and rain. Engine bleed air is ducted to the one-piece rain removal manifold at the base of the windshield. Two cable guide rails associated with the cable cutter flank the windshield's center panel. (Lennart Lundh)

The lower cable cutter of the AH-1S's cable strike protection kit is mounted immediately forward of the M28 turret. The cutter is bolted to a base plate, which itself is bolted to the airframe. This cutter has a sharp angle to sever telephone or electrical power cables, preventing the cables from damaging the helicopter. (Lennart Lundh)

A grab handle for cockpit access help is attached to the forward cockpit's front canopy frame. The standby compass placed forward of this handle provides bearing information in the event the main compass located on the instrument panel fails. A rearview mirror is located on the starboard frame. (Keith Lovern)

AH-1S cockpit interiors are painted Flat Black for low reflectivity while using Night Vision Goggles (NVGs). Seat upholstery is a light green (approximately FS34373) with light tan (approximately FS37886) seat belts. The hose for providing warm or cool air from the Environmental Control Unit is placed on the seat back. Emergency canopy removal system cables are attached to the sloped instrument panel between the cockpits. (Keith Lovern)

The AH-1S gunner/copilot's telescopic sight is fitted to the center of the instrument panel and corresponds to the nose-mounted Telescopic Sight Unit (TSU). Grips with triggers are incorporated into each side of the sight. A portable Grimes cockpit light is attached to the seat's starboard armor panel. The striped handle near the cyclic control stick activates the emergency canopy removal system. (Keith Lovern)

An XM-73 reflector sight, more common to the AH-1G, is mounted to the pilot's instrument panel of this AH-1S. This sight allows the pilot to aim the weapons when they are not under the gunner/copilot's control. A radar warning indicator (large circular screen) and a torque meter for displaying engine torque are added atop the panel. (Keith Lovern)

21

This AH-1S (68-15157) was assigned to the 1st Squadron, 167th Air Cavalry of the Nebraska National Guard. Its turret weapons and ammunition drums are removed, allowing carriage of other cargo. The large open panel exposes the transmission and first stage of the engine. Wing-mounted armament consists of two-cell TOW launchers outboard and seven-tube XM-157 rocket launchers inboard. (Butch Lottman)

Large access panels on the starboard side expose the AH-1S's turboshaft engine and transmission. A bipod mount helps secure the engine combustion chamber to the engine bay. The oval Plexiglas window in the lower transmission access panel allows ground crews to check the transmission oil sight gauge without opening the panel. (Butch Lottman)

The port engine and transmission access panels are open on this AH-1S. The forward access panel covers the transmission and engine air inlet section. The open aft panel reveals the 1800 SHP Avco Lycoming T53-L-703 turboshaft engine. A rectangular armor plate over the engine access door protects vital fuel controls. (Carmelo D. Turdo)

The port transmission access door of the AH-1S is connected to a tubular hinged frame. Inner surfaces of access doors are painted with Zinc Chromate (FS33814) anti-corrosion paint. The T53-L-703 engine is removed from this aircraft; normally, it is mounted aft of the transmission. (Author)

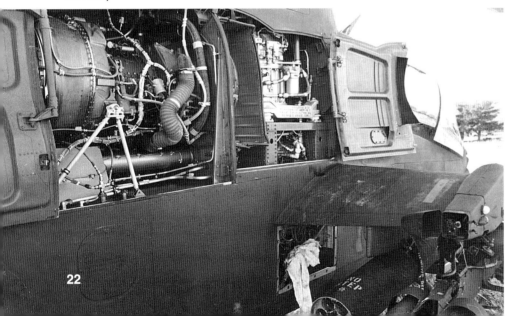

The AH-1S's engine exhaust outlet is located on the engine compartment's aft section. The rounded attachment atop the exhaust fairing helps reduce the Infrared (IR) signature by preventing airflow from forcing hot exhaust downward, away from the rotor wash. The tail rotor drive shaft is exposed through the screened openings at the exhaust section base. (Author)

A flush-mounted radio altimeter antenna is mounted on the lower fuselage, under the engine compartment. This instrument uses radio waves to precisely measure the Cobra's altitude. The oval intake for the Environmental Control System (ECS) helps cool electrical equipment in the lower port fuselage compartment. The small door aft of the intake covers a ground power unit receptacle. (Lennart Lundh)

A target acquisition panel was retrofitted to the AH-1S's lower fuselage. This required relocating the landing light from the forward undersurface to the skid support tube. Ground handling wheels are attached to the skid undercarriage for manual maneuvering of the Cobra. Sway braces fitted to the undersurface of the stub wing pylons prevent ordnance from swaying to port or starboard during flight. (Author)

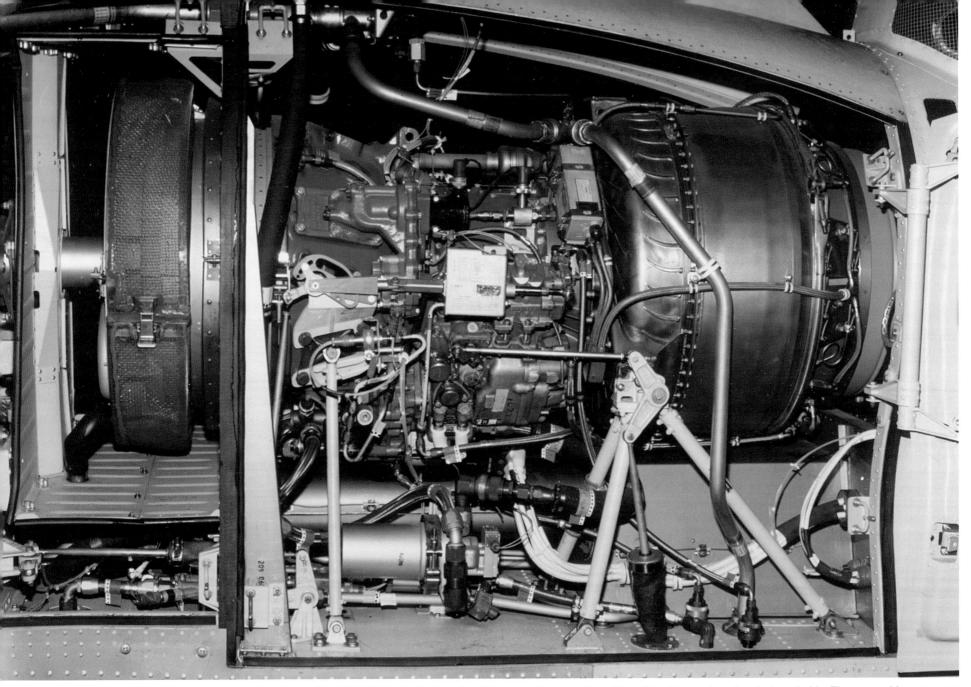

The AH-1S is powered by an 1800 SHP Avco Lycoming T53-L-703 turboshaft engine. This was an upgraded version of the same manufacturer's 1400 SHP T53-L-13 fitted to the earlier AH-1G. A tripod and single mount secure the engine to the engine deck on the aircraft's port side, while a bipod is used on the starboard side. The removable screen on the inlet section allows cleaning of the filter elements, preventing FOD to the engine. (Bell)

Single engine Cobras feature recessed inlets on both sides, which channel air to the engine compressor. The oval window immediately below the inlet is the transmission oil level sight gauge, while an auxiliary inlet scoop is placed aft of the intake. The engine oil filler is located in the rotor pylon and is behind the rectangular access panel. (Lennart Lundh)

An armor panel attached to the engine access door of the AH-1S protects vital engine controls. Fire sensing elements, attached to these doors on the AH-1G, were relocated within the engine compartment of the AH-1S. Access door and equipment bay interiors are painted Zinc Chromate (FS33814) to prevent corrosion. (C.M. Rood)

AH-1S rotor head components are painted a light gray (approximately FS36495). The push-pull tubes flanking the rotor mast transfer pilot control input from the collective stick to the rotor blades. A dark gray cover normally protects the leading edge braces; however, the cover is removed from this Cobra. (C.M. Reed)

A black plastic cover is placed inside the exhaust section of this AH-1S. This cover prevents FOD from entering the aft engine section while the Cobra is on the ground. The screened openings at the base of the tail rotor drive shaft tunnel vents heat from the engine deck. The heat-dissipating exhaust extension has been removed from this aircraft. Exhausts are cooled by the rotor wash, reducing the helicopter's IR signature. (Lennart Lundh)

The AH-1S stub wings have a combined span of 10 feet 9 inches (3.3 m). The earlier AH-1G's stub wing span was 10 feet 4 inches (3.1 m). TOW units on all Cobra models through the AH-1W are mounted on the outboard wing station, which has two pairs of sway braces. The inner station of this AH-1S, which usually carries rocket pods, has an additional sway brace mounted on its inboard side. (Author)

A four-tube TOW launcher is mounted on this AH-1S's outboard stub wing station, while a 19-tube XM-200 rocket launcher is fitted to the inboard station. Both launchers are empty of their weapons. The forward fairing for the outboard wing station was removed on this Cobra, exposing the forward ordnance attachment mechanism. (Lennart Lundh)

The nonskid walking area on this AH-1S's stub wing stops short of both the leading and trailing edges. This marks the safe areas for which air and ground crews can stand on the wing. The panel behind the canopy covers the hydraulic reservoir and Environmental Control Unit compartment. A folded tarpaulin is placed inside the open turret ammunition bay. (Author)

Black non-skid paint marks the walk area of this AH-1S's stub wing. The outboard TOW mount's upper surface has a distinct airfoil shape. A step for access to and from the stub wing is attached to the aft skid support. (Lennart Lundh)

An oil level sight gauge is mounted where the dorsal spine meets the tail fin leading edge on all Cobras. A wire loop connects the chip detector in front of this gauge to the 42° gear box, which is incorporated into the tail rotor drive shaft. A Loral AN/APR-38 radar warning antenna is placed beneath the DANGER arrow, while a white position light is mounted further aft. This antenna and light arrangement is repeated on the port side. (Lennart Lundh)

The Cobra's tail rotor pitch is controlled by input through a control rod in the mounting shaft. Input from the tail rotor control pedals in the cockpit adjusts the pitch as required. Counterweights flanking the mounting shaft on this AH-1S – and other Cobra variants – maintain neutral pitch. (Lennart Lundh)

A tapered fairing covers the 90° gear box for the AH-1S tail rotor. The tail rotor's motion is synchronized with the main rotor, preventing either rotor from striking the other. The hollow steel tail skid is standard on all Cobras to protect the tail rotor from tail-low landings. This AH-1S was not equipped with an AN/APR-38 radar warning antenna on the tail boom. The strap extending from the tail boom is wrapped around the end of the main rotor blade, preventing it from 'windmilling' while the helicopter was parked. (Author)

The TOW missile system enables the Cobra to attack heavy armor and fortified targets. TOW launchers hold two or four BGM-71 missiles, which are loaded in their factory-sealed tubes. After the maintenance-free launchers are secured to the wing stations, electrical firing cables are connected to the missiles. (Lennart Lundh)

A four-tube TOW launcher is mounted on the port outboard pylon of this AH-1S stub wing, while a 19-tube XM-200 rocket launcher is placed on the inboard pylon. The aft end of the TOW launcher is lowered for loading the missile tube into the launch position, then it is raised to the horizontal position. (Lennart Lundh)

The TOW launcher's center section contains the unit's main support members and electrical connections. Missile launch and guidance commands are sent from the cockpit to the missile through these connections. A 19-tube XM-200 rocket pod is installed beside the TOW launcher. (Lennart Lundh)

Two pairs of sway braces help secure the XM-200 rocket pod to the inboard stub wing pylon. An additional sway brace is fitted to the wing undersurface. Two mooring rings are mounted at the wing root and are used to secure the Cobra to the ground when parked for extended periods. (Lennart Lundh)

Two modernized AH-1S Cobras prepare to take off during training in 1988. Both aircraft were retrofitted with flat-plate canopies and 20MM General Electric M197 three-barrel cannon in the lower nose turret. The Cobra in the foreground is equipped with the interim Infrared (IR) reducing exhaust nozzle and airflow baffle. A Frequency Modulation (FM) homing antenna is mounted aft of the upper cable cutter. (US Army)

A small number of modernized AH-1S Cobras equip Thailand's Attack Aviation Battalion, including this example (9998) armed with TOW missiles. The extended exhaust nozzle retrofitted to this Cobra became standard on the later AH-1F. The nozzle reduces exhaust heat through controlled radiation, reducing the aircraft's IR signature. A Tracor M-130 chaff/flare dispenser mounted on the tail protects the Cobra from radar-directed antiaircraft weapons and IR-guided missiles. (Bell)

The second AH-1P (76-22568) was originally called the AH-1S (PROD), for 'Production.' The AH-1P followed the AH-1Q and introduced the seven-piece flat plate canopy, which reduced glint and radar signature over the previous bubble canopy. This new canopy also resulted in enlarged cockpit space for both crewmen. The AH-1P also featured a new navigation package and an improved instrument panel. (Bell)

29

The 7.62MM M134 Minigun and 40MM M129 grenade launcher are removed from this AH-1P of the 1st Squadron, 167th Air Cavalry, Nebraska National Guard in 1991. A technician cleans the six barrels of the 7.62MM weapon. Next to the M134 is a bullet trap, which is fitted over the muzzle when the Minigun is installed. This trap is necessary since hand rotating the barrels can fire the Minigun. The 7.62MM ammunition drum has been placed on the lowered ammunition bay door. (Butch Lottman)

The AH-1P's Emerson M28 turret incorporates an electrically operated 7.62MM GE M134 Minigun to starboard and a 40MM Hughes M129 grenade launcher to port. This is the same turret fitted to the earlier AH-1G and AH-1S variants. Port and starboard turret covers are replaced after the weapons are installed. (Butch Lottman)

A Nebraska National Guard technician services an AH-1P's 40MM M129 grenade launcher in 1991. The 231-round 40MM ammunition drum is fully extended on the compartment door. These weapons are thoroughly cleaned to remove gunpowder residue from the barrels and excess grease from the firing mechanism. (Butch Lottman)

A technician performs maintenance on the 7.62MM ammunition drum. Drums for the Minigun and grenade launcher ammunition easily slide out of the bay onto the opened access door. A two-tube TOW launcher and a seven-tube XM-157 rocket pod are mounted on the starboard stub wing. (Butch Lottman)

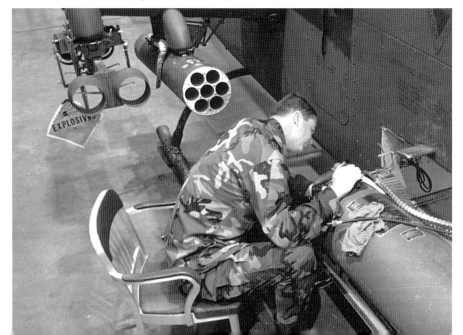

The grenade launcher ammunition drum has been taken from this AH-1P for maintenance. The removed port access panels reveal the ammunition chute and control system links. Fuselage access panels are taken off to conduct a thorough inspection required every 100 flight hours. (Butch Lottman)

The AH-1P is powered by a 1800 SHP Avco Lycoming T53-L-703 turboshaft engine, which also equips the earlier AH-1S. The air inlet section is mounted ahead of the engine, with the transmission forward of the inlet. The transmission base rests atop a sturdy metal frame and incorporates vibration dampers. The dampers reduce rotor-induced vibration so it is not transmitted beyond the rotor mast and linkage into the fuselage and flight controls. (Butch Lottman)

The US Marine Corps (USMC) met success with their AH-1G Cobras in Vietnam and ordered a more heavily armed, twin-engine version. Work on the AH-1J SeaCobra began in 1968 and resulted in a Cobra slightly larger than the AH-1G. Modifications for Marine use included a wider chord tail rotor, a strengthened and lengthened tail fin, a rotor brake, Navy electronics, and the 20MM XM197 three-barrel cannon. Installation of an 1800 SHP Pratt & Whitney PT6T-4 Twin Pac turboshaft engine required extensive redesign of the engine fairings and rotor pylon. This Cobra (BuNo 157758) is the second AH-1J built, armed with 19-tube XM-200 rocket pods on the stub wings. The USMC AH-1J was Bell's first twin-engine Cobra and the first with air-to-air capability. It entered service in 1969, in time for combat trials in Vietnam. (Bell)

The fourth AH-1J (BuNo 157760) departs from a ship during sea trials. It is equipped with orange nose and rotor mast instruments for the tests. A seven-tube XM-157 rocket pod is mounted under the starboard wing. The 69 AH-1Js produced were factory-painted flat Field Green (FS34095), with Dark Gull Gray (FS36231) interiors. (Bell)

The battery compartment is located in the AH-1J's nose and is accessed via the rectangular panel on the upper nose surface. The pitot tube – used to gather airspeed data for cockpit instruments – is located at the nose tip, flanked by the Radar Homing and Warning (RHAW) antennas to port and starboard. (Lennart Lundh)

The AH-1J introduced a chin turret equipped with the 20mm General Electric XM197 cannon. The three-barrel weapon fires up to 3000 rounds per minute. This met the USMC's requirements for greater firepower than the AH-1G, which had a turret-mounted 7.62mm machine gun. A cable cutter is mounted just forward of the turret. (Lennart Lundh)

The AH-1J pilot's seat is fitted with large boron carbide side armor panels, which help protect the pilot from enemy fire. A map and logbook holder is attached to this Cobra's port side armor panel. Smaller armor panels are fitted to the gunner/copilot's seat, due to the more confined space of the forward cockpit. (Lennart Lundh)

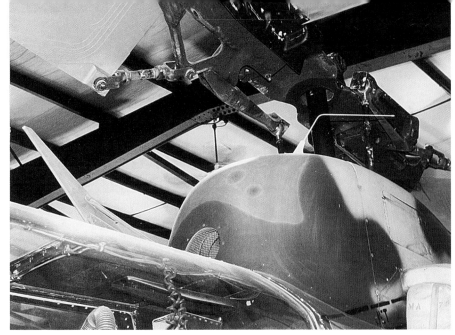

AH-1Js painted the land camouflage scheme of Blue Gray (FS35237), Black (FS37038), and Field Green (FS34095) have dark gray (approximately FS36176) and black rotor heads. A round screened cooling vent is centered at the rotor pylon's leading edge. The cable cutter mounted above the canopy severs telephone and power lines in flight. (Lennart Lundh)

The AH-1J's engine intakes flank the upper center fuselage. The upward angled intakes collect air free from the majority of sea spray and other potential Foreign Object Damage (FOD). What is believed to be the Vietnam Service Medal ribbon is painted on the intake. (Lennart Lundh)

A large air inlet feeds each of the AH-1J's engines. An anti-FOD cover is placed inside the port inlet to prevent FOD to the engine while the aircraft is parked in its hangar. Stenciling on the vented hydraulic reservoir panel just forward of the intake indicates the rotor brake master cylinder is inside. The Marines required a rotor brake on their Cobras to immediately stop the rotors from turning after engine shut down aboard ship. (Lennart Lundh)

The ordnance displayed with this AH-1T illustrates the range of firepower available to all Marine Cobras, including the earlier AH-1J. Four 19-tube 2.75 inch (70MM) LAU-61 rocket pods are mounted on the Sea Cobra's stub wings. Breakaway fairings on the pods provide aerodynamic covering for the rockets and are jettisoned during firing. Four more LAU-61s pods are placed immediately ahead of the aircraft, with four seven-tube LAU-68 pods ahead of the LAU-61s. Thirty-two BGM-71 TOW missiles — 16 per side – flank the rocket pods, while CBU-55 Fuel Air Explosive (FAE) bombs are outboard of the TOWs. Placed ahead of the TOW missiles are 2.75 inch rockets. Flanking the M118 grenade dispenser in front of the rocket pods are eight grenades. Eight Mk 45 parachute flares are placed outside of the grenades to the left, while eight Mk 115 practice bombs are lined up to the right. In the front are two 7.62MM SUU-11 Minigun pods, with 20MM ammunition belts to the right and 7.62MM ammunition belts to the left. (Bell)

This AH-1J is experimentally fitted with a twin launcher for General Dynamics MIM-43 Redeye Surface-to-Air Missiles (SAMs) on specially modified wing mounts. The Redeye was a shoulder-launched heat-seeking SAM that entered service in the mid-1960s. This missile was used to test arming SeaCobras for air-to-air combat against enemy helicopters. The Redeye was not adopted for Cobras; however, the later AH-1W can carry two Ford Aerospace AIM-9L Sidewinder Air-to-Air Missiles (AAMs) for self-defense purposes. Streamlined fairings cover the AH-1J's tubular skid supports to minimize drag. Each skid incorporates an access step on the leading edge. The AH-1J's canopy handles are not flush mounted, unlike those fitted to the earlier AH-1G. (Bell)

AH-1Js have three flush air inlets in each engine cowling. These inlets assist in cooling both engine compartments. The cowling panels are removed during engine maintenance. (Lennart Lundh)

The AH-1J's side-by-side engine exhausts are mounted high on the engine compartment. This arrangement results in the compartment's blunt aft side. No Infrared (IR)-reducing exhaust nozzles were fitted to the AH-1J. An oil radiator is placed beneath the two exhausts. (Lennart Lundh)

The AH-1J has access steps built into the forward and aft landing skid supports. An additional step is mounted just below the wing trailing edge to assist the pilot onto the wing walkway area. Black non-skid surfaces are placed on the skid leading edge beside the step and on the wing walkway. An additional stores support mechanism is fitted to the inboard wing pylon to help prevent ordnance from swaying in flight. (Bell)

35

The starboard stub wing of the AH-1J has a green navigation light at the leading edge of a side-mounted teardrop-shaped fairing. Light yellow Night Vision Goggle (NVG) light strips applied to the outer wing upper surfaces help pilots maintain sight of the aircraft during night operations. Walkway areas atop the wing varied significantly in size and color. (Lennart Lundh)

A red light is fitted to the teardrop-shaped fairing on the AH-1J's port stub wing. Two pairs of sway braces fitted to the outboard pylon secure stores in place during flight. The trailing edge of the tapered wingtip fairing is hinged for access to electrical firing connectors. The Cobra's stub wings help provide some additional lift in horizontal flight. (Lennart Lundh)

A large structural brace is fitted high inside each engine air inlet flanking the AH-1J's engine compartment. Air is ingested above and below this brace for the engine compartment. Inlet interiors are painted glossy Insignia White (FS17875) to aid visibility in the tunnel-like channel. The intake lip is painted the same color as the surrounding airframe – in this case, glossy Field Green (FS14097). (Lennart Lundh)

A sturdy angled stores rack is fitted to the inboard wing station of an AH-1J. This rack is used when the SeaCobra carries heavy armament on the wings, including the CBU-55 Fuel-Air Explosive (FAE) bomb. AH-1Js use FAE bombs to clear minefields and destroy underground bunker complexes. (Lennart Lundh)

The inboard wing station rack is fitted with one-piece sway braces at its fore and aft ends. Two prongs on the ordnance slide into catches within openings placed near the sway braces. One firing cable enters the center of the rack upper surface, while a second cable is attached to the aft end. (Lennart Lundh)

A cockpit access step is attached to the forward edge of the AH-1J's skid supports. Another step is placed on the fuselage for the use of pilots and technicians requiring access to the upper fuselage and stub wings. Mooring rings for securing the SeaCobra to the ship's deck are fitted on the undersurface and skid tips. (Lennart Lundh)

A fire extinguisher is mounted inside this hinged panel on the AH-1J's port side below the engine. The extinguisher's dry chemical contents are directed into various openings in the engine compartment. The small hatch aft of the fire extinguisher door covers an external power receptacle, which is used when the helicopter is on the ground. (Lennart Lundh)

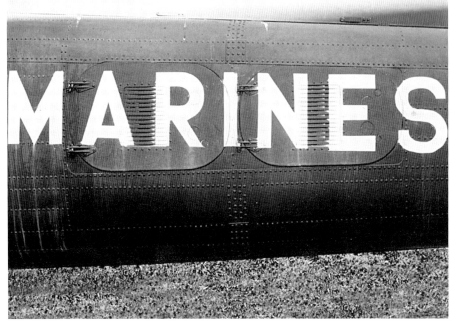

The radio access panel is mounted on the AH-1J's starboard fuselage below the engine compartment. Two columns of vents are placed inside the panel to allow air heated by the radio equipment to escape the compartment. Eight round head screws fasten the compartment in place. (Lennart Lundh)

All Cobras have mechanically controlled elevators to enhance trim. The AH-1J elevator – introduced on the earlier AH-1Q – spans 6 feet 11 inches (2.1 м), a nine inch (22.9 см) increase over the AH-1G's elevator span. This larger elevator is standard on all late Cobra variants. The elevator is manually adjusted in one of three positions, depending upon the center of gravity (CG) or trim requirements. (Lennart Lundh)

Two vented hinged panels are placed along the port side of the AH-1J's tail boom. These panels provide access to the tail rotor linkage and miscellaneous components. The dorsal housing above the tail boom houses the tail rotor transmission shaft. (Lennart Lundh)

A single fairing is mounted on each side of the late model AH-1J's aft tail boom. This fairing houses a navigation light (top), a position light (aft), and a radar warning antenna (side). The antenna warns the crew of enemy surface-based and air-based radars tracking the SeaCobra. A fiberglass tailcone covers the end of the metal tail boom. (Lennart Lundh)

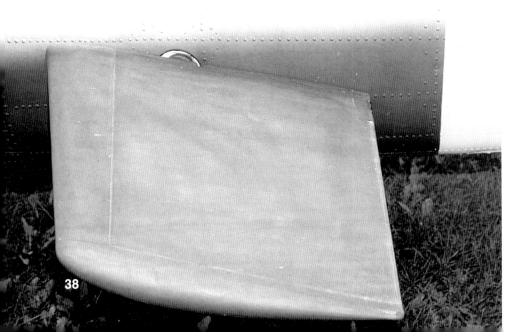

This early model AH-1J has a position light on the aft portion of the tail boom. Navigation lights and radar warning antennas were not installed in this fairing at the time. The hinged cover over the 42° gearbox has a cutout for checking the unit's oil level sight gauge. (Lennart Lundh)

The AH-1J tail rotor hub incorporates feathering and pitch control linkage. A bulbous tapered fairing normally covers the 90° gearbox. Tail rotors were relocated to the starboard side of the tail of AH-1Gs to improve directional control. The starboard tail rotor installation became standard on all later Cobras through the AH-1W SuperCobra. (Lennart Lundh)

The early AH-1J tail boom had a white position light fitted to the port side; an identical light was also fitted to starboard. This light – and the red (port) and green (starboard) position lights – are usually turned on for non-combat flying at night and in bad weather. Lights are usually turned off during night combat missions. (Lennart Lundh)

Tail rotor actuator rod links extend from the port side of the 90° gearbox. This actuator passes through the center of the tail rotor shaft. The fastener pattern aft of the linkage opening outlines the shape of the gearbox fairing on the opposite side. (Lennart Lundh)

(Left) The Enhanced Cobra Armament System (ECAS), or 'Up-Gun Cobra,' preceded the AH-1F. Redesignated the AH-1E, it introduced composite rotor blades, a Rocket Management System (RMS), and a heavier and more advanced 20MM turret. This AH-1E (21507) makes a test flight from Bell's Arlington, Texas flight test facility. The cannon barrels are not fitted to the GE universal turret under the nose. Four-tube TOW missile launchers are mounted from the port outboard wing station. This Cobra was later the first of two AH-1Es sent to Japan in April of 1979, prior to Fuji license-building the AH-1F for the Japan Ground Self-Defense Force from 1984. Bell produced 98 AH-1Es for the US Army during 1979. (Bell)

(Below) Barely identifiable as an early AH-1G (66-15266), this AH-1F, nicknamed PHOENIX, carries a lethal array of armament. TOW launchers are mounted on the outboard wing stations, 19-tube 2.75 inch (70MM) M261 rocket pods are fitted on the inboard wing stations, and the 20MM XM197 cannon is under the nose. The nose-mounted Telescopic Sight Unit (TSU) is turned to port, revealing the nose deflector of the cable strike protection system. (Werner Roth)

(Below) The AH-1F, or Modernized Cobra, is the result of steady improvements to the AH-1S line. Deliveries of this variant – the Army's ultimate Cobra – began in 1979. Major changes over previous models include a cockpit Heads-Up Display (HUD), an Infrared (IR) engine exhaust suppressor, and an IR jammer atop the engine compartment. Other changes include a laser range finder, Doppler navigation system, RMS, a fire control computer, and closed-circuit fueling. This AH-1F hover taxis at Osan Air Base, Korea in 1984. (Tom Maloney)

The US Army deployed a number of AH-1Fs to Saudi Arabia during Operation DESERT SHIELD in 1990-91, including this Cobra (67-15512). Many of these Cobras were painted Sand (FS33717) over the standard Helo Drab camouflage. The main rotor heads and markings remained Flat Black (FS37038). The black upward-pointed chevron painted on the engine intake is a Coalition forces recognition symbol, which was also painted on armored vehicles. This AH-1F is equipped with a 19-tube M261 Folding Fin Aircraft Rockets (FFAR) launcher in the inboard stub wing. A four-tube launcher for Hughes BGM-71 TOW (Tube-launched, Optically-tracked, Wire-guided) anti-armor missiles is mounted on the outboard wing pylon. Cobras served alongside McDonnell Douglas (now Boeing) AH-64 Apaches during the DESERT SHIELD and the subsequent Operation DESERT STORM war against Iraq in early 1991. (Werner Roth)

SAND SHARK is an AH-1F (67-15643) assigned to N Troop, 4th Squadron, 2nd Armored Cavalry Regiment during Operation DESERT STORM. The Cobra is parked at a forward operating location in Iraq on 28 February 1991. The aircraft is painted overall Sand with black main rotor heads and markings, including a sharkmouth and eyes on the forward fuselage. The two-cell launchers are loaded with BGM-71 TOW missiles. Only a few 2.75 inch (70MM) FFARs are in the 19-tube M261 launcher.

(Below) Another AH-1F deployed to the Persian Gulf was this Cobra (67-15659). The Sand paint applied over the standard Helo Drab finish for Operations DESERT SHIELD and DESERT STORM shows sign of wear on the rotor pylon, mid-fuselage, and tail fin. Painted in black under the gunner/copilot's canopy is CW2 LVI "THE CUDA." CW2 stood for Chief Warrant Officer 2 – the gunner/copilot's rank – but the meaning of LVI is unknown. "THE CUDA" appears to have been this warrant officer's nickname. The AH-1F is parked at a stateside Army airfield following DESERT STORM. (Werner Roth)

(Above) This AH-1F (80-23510) makes a pre-delivery test flight from Bell's Arlington facility. Bell and Avco Lycoming jointly developed the IR suppressor exhaust section, which was first mounted on late AH-1S Cobras. Controlled radiation of the heated exhaust gases cools the exhaust and reduces the helicopter's IR signature. Two notable changes introduced by the AH-1F are the low airspeed data sensor projecting from the cockpit frame, and the ball-shaped laser tracker at the front of the rotor pylon. After the Vietnam War, US Army Cobras are painted overall Helo Drab (FS34031). (Bell)

The AH-1F is armed with the 20MM General Electric (GE) XM197 cannon, which is fitted in a GE Universal Turret Subsystem (UTS) under the nose. The three-barrel M197's firing rate ranges from 680 to 780 rounds per minute (RPM), with 730 RPM as its nominal firing rate. The electrically-powered UTS has an elevation range of +20.5°/-50° and can be slewed 110° to either port or starboard. The gunner/copilot in the front cockpit fires the XM197 using either the Telescopic Sighting Unit (TSU) or the Helmet Sighting Subsystem (HSS). The pilot can fire the weapon in either the flexible or fixed (stowed forward) modes using the HSS. US Army Cobras seldom use the protective cover over the turret drive and recoil assemblies. (Butch Lottman)

The XM197 three-barrel cannon used on the AH-1F was first installed on the US Marine Corps' AH-1J SeaCobra in 1969. The weapon is based on GE's 20MM M61 Vulcan six-barrel cannon used by many US combat aircraft. A motor driven mechanism on the starboard side feeds ammunition through flexible chutes to the cannon's breech assembly. (Bell)

The AH-1F ammunition container slides out onto the opened compartment door for easy loading. Two cables extending from inside the compartment support the opened door. Large grab handles and loading instructions are placed on the outboard side. This container holds 750 rounds of 20MM ammunition for the XM197 cannon. (Butch Lottman)

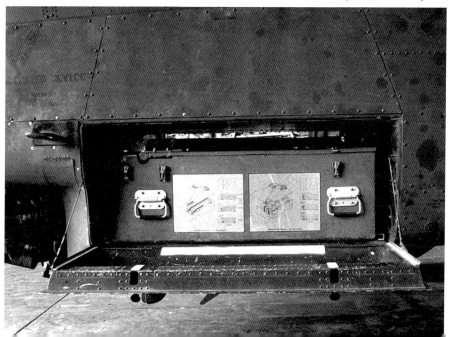

Ground crewmen load 20MM ammunition belts onto an AH-1S assigned to the 229th Attack Helicopter Battalion, 101st Airborne Division (Air Assault) in 1984. The ammunition container has two parallel bays for storing ammunition for the XM197 cannon. An improved 19-tube 2.75 inch M261 lightweight rocket launcher, which replaced the original XM-200 pod, is mounted on the inboard wing pylon, while a TOW launcher is fitted to the outboard pylon. (US Army)

43

Both AH-1F cockpit doors are opened: the gunner/copilot's to port, the pilot's to starboard. A gas-operated strut keeps each door open and retracts when the door is closed. Two-cell TOW launchers and seven-tube 2.75 inch M260 rocket launchers are mounted under the stub wings. The latter replaced the Vietnam era XM-157/158 rocket launchers. (Sean M. Borland)

The M65 Telescopic Sighting Unit (TSU) for aiming the Cobra's weapons is mounted in a nose turret. A small fairing aft of this turret houses a Radar Homing And Warning (RHAW) antenna; this antenna is also fitted to the starboard nose and to the port and starboard tail. US Army AH-1s seldom use the protective cover of the 20MM XM197 three-barreled cannon. A step for the gunner/copilot projects from the fuselage side. (Terry Love)

This Korea-based AH-1F and other successive Cobra variants retain the narrow profile of the original AH-1G. The later AH-1F is fitted with slightly bulged canopy side panels for increased cockpit room. This variant changed the canopy from the original bubble design to one with flat plates, which reduces glint from light striking the Plexiglas. The air data sensor is placed on a tube projecting from the upper canopy. The composite main rotor blades introduced on the AH-1E 'Up-Gun Cobra' have a reduced radar signature over the previous metal rotor blades. The newer blades are also more apt to maintain their structural integrity when damaged. (Sean M. Borland)

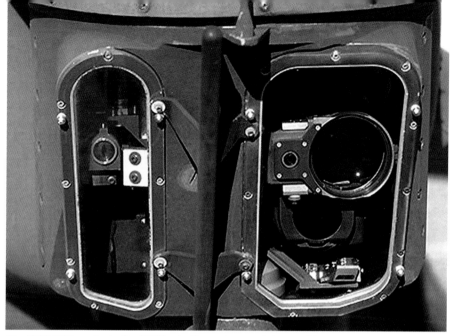

The M65 TSU controls the TOW missile system and the position of the Universal Turret System (UTS) through helmet sights worn by both crewmen. A laser rangefinder is fitted in the nose turret to starboard of the TSU. The rod attached between the TSU's sight panels deflects wires to a wire cutter just forward of the turret. (Frank White)

This DESERT STORM era AH-1F, TRIGGER AND BOOMER'S EXCELLENT ADVENTURE, is equipped with updated RHAW antennas on the nose. The canopy frame remained Helo Drab on the overall Sand painted Cobra. The bulge below the canopy gives the gunner/copilot room to move his side-mounted cyclic (directional control) stick. (Werner Roth)

The AH-1S and later AH-1F essentially became a night fighter with the development of the Hughes Cobra-Nite (C-Nite) Targeting System. Fielded during the late 1980s, C-Nite permits target acquisition and weapons firing in darkness, as well as in smoke, haze, and bad weather. This sight uses a laser range finder and is based on the earlier M65 TSU. (Sean M. Borland)

The AH-1F's four RHAW antennas – including this one on the port nose – correspond to the Singer AN/APR-39(V)1 Radar Warning Receiver. This provides both visual and audio warnings in the cockpit, showing the range and azimuth of search and fire control radar systems targeting the Cobra. (Author)

The Boresight Assembly Ground Support Equipment (BAGSE) boresighter was introduced for the Modernized Cobra (AH-1F). The yellow nose-mounted device is portable and is used for precision 20MM cannon calibration day or night, either indoors or outdoors, and on uneven surfaces. The BAGSE is fitted to an AH-1F of the 2nd Aviation Battalion, 2nd Infantry Division at Camp Casey, Korea in 1984. (Tom Maloney)

The air data sensor projects significantly from the starboard side of the AH-1F's canopy frame. This sensor feeds outside air data – both airspeed and direction – to the Teledyne fire control computer for optimum weapons accuracy. High winds can otherwise degrade weapons accuracy, particularly for rockets and missiles. (David Roof)

US Army pilot Sean M. Borland stands beside his Korea-based AH-1F, the top-of-the-line Cobra variant in Army service. The 20MM XM197 cannon fires at a nominal rate of 730 RPM with an effective range of over 2000 M (6561.7 feet). Ammunition types available to the XM197 include Armor Piercing Incendiary (API), High Explosive Incendiary (HEI), High Explosive Incendiary Tracer (HEIT), and Armor Piercing Incendiary (API). (Sean M. Borland)

The pilot's Heads-Up Display (HUD) is placed atop the instrument panel of this AH-1F. The HUD presents essential flight and weapons data at eye level. This DESERT STORM veteran illustrates that personal markings made a significant comeback during the 1991 Middle East conflict. (Werner Roth)

The AH-1F's ventral wire cutter and support braces are fitted to the forward fuselage, below the pilot's cockpit. A landing light is folded back immediately in front of the wire cutter. This light extends down during landing to illuminate the landing zone for the flight crew. (Author)

Wide canopy framing reveals this AH-1F's origin as an early AH-1S. Late production AH-1S Cobras have narrow canopy frames with slightly bulged cockpit windows. The inner surfaces of this display aircraft's windows were painted black to preserve the cockpit from the sun's damaging ultraviolet rays. The air-operated rain removal system's manifold consists of seven individual ports located at the windshield base. (Author)

The AH-1F uses a projecting canopy handle, which replaces the flush-mounted handles fitted to some early Cobra models. Black stenciling under the gunner/copilot's canopy warns flight and ground crews about the canopy removal system's explosive materials. A step for the gunner/copilot is located below this stenciling. (David Roof)

The hydraulic reservoir is located aft of the pilot's cockpit. Spilled hydraulic liquid discolors the low radar reflective Helo Drab (FS34031) paint applied to US Army combat aircraft. A vent placed within the access panel includes a reservoir liquid level sight gauge, which is viewed from outside the aircraft. (David Roof)

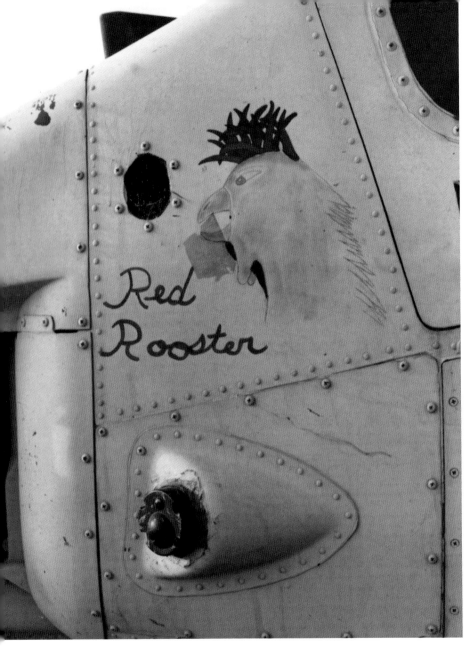

The AH-1F pilot's instrument panel is nearly identical to that of the earlier AH-1S. Ventilation ports are incorporated into the instrument shroud sides. Primary flight instruments are placed in the panel's center section, with engine and armament controls on the lower port side. The master caution light panel is installed on the lower starboard panel. The cockpits of later AH-1s are Flat Black (FS37038), which offers reduced reflectivity at night over the previously used Dark Gull Gray (FS36231). (Sean M. Borland)

The AH-1F's pilot has a Heads Up Display (HUD) mounted atop the instrument shroud. Vital flight and targeting information is projected onto the angled glass, which is placed at the pilot's eye level. HUD controls are placed immediately below the angled glass. Rails mounted along the upper port canopy connect the aircrew's helmets to the Helmet Sight Subsystem (HSS), which enables either crewman to swiftly acquire targets by looking at them. (Sean M. Borland)

An AN/APR-39(V)1 Radar Warning Receiver (RWR) antenna is mounted on the port nose of *Red Rooster*, an AH-1F which saw action during Operation DESERT STORM in 1991. RWR antennas placed on the Cobra's four quadrants alert the pilot to hostile radars tracking his aircraft. The vent beside the nose art was created in the field during DESERT STORM. This provided additional cooling of avionics located in this section under the desert conditions of the Arabian peninsula. (Werner Roth)

The rotor head components of modern Cobras are Flat Black, instead of the light gray used on earlier variants. The Airborne Laser Tracker (ALT) designator fairing is molded into the rotor pylon's leading edge. This tracker is used to seek and track targets that are designated by an external laser designator. The 9 and 1 with crossed sabers on the rotor pylon designate the 9th Squadron, 1st Cavalry Regiment. (Author)

The AH-1F featured an improved filtration system in the air inlets, which helped cope with sand conditions during Operation DESERT STORM. Fire control system components are housed within the teardrop-shaped bulge just forward of the inlet. A red anti-collision light is mounted atop the rotor pylon, aft of the main rotor shaft. (Werner Roth)

Two large doors on both the port and starboard sides provide access to the transmission and engine on all Army Cobras. Technicians removed the aft door and the panel beneath this AH-1F's exhaust section during extended maintenance. The AH-1F – formerly AH-1S (Modernized) – is powered by one 1800 SHP Avco Lycoming T53-L-703 turboshaft engine. The powerplant is 47.6 inches (120.9 CM) long, with a maximum diameter of 23 inches (58.4 CM) and a weight of 540 pounds (244.9 KG). Power from the engine is sent to the transmission, which transfers this power to the main rotor. (Tom Maloney)

The engine inlet flow diverter has four structural ribs running lengthwise along the side. A small fin added to the diverter's aft section aids in airflow management. An auxiliary inlet is placed aft of the flow diverter. (David Roof)

The Sanders AN/ALQ-144 active Infrared (IR) jamming unit is mounted atop the exhaust section of AH-1S variants. It sends heat pulses away from the aircraft, countering heat-seeking missiles. The IR suppressing exhaust nozzle is removed from this aircraft. The entire exhaust section is well vented for optimum cooling. (David Roof)

This AH-1S is equipped with an engine inlet flow diverter. Air enters the inlet only through the open upper portion of this device. The inlet flow diverter permits a hovering Cobra to fire the Mk 66 Wrap-Around-Fin Aircraft Rocket (WAFAR), which replaced the earlier Mk 4 and Mk 40 Folding Fin Aircraft Rockets (FFARs). Initial hover firing of the more powerful Mk 66 resulted in a partial vacuum near the inlet, which robbed the engine of necessary air flow and caused compressor stalls. (David Roof)

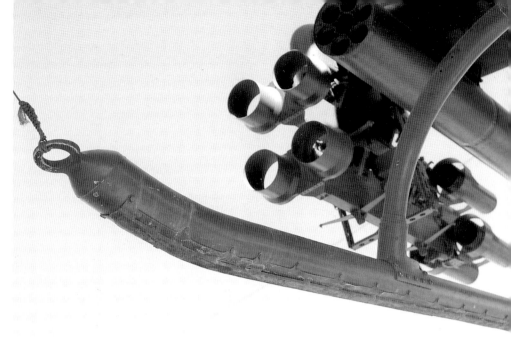

Two pairs of arched landing skid supports running from the lower fuselage support each AH-1 landing skid. Metal shoes are attached to the bottom of all Cobra landing skids. A landing light is mounted on the forward support for the port skid on this AH-1F. The robust skids absorb the energy generated in high sink rate landings. (Author)

Support bracing is attached to the inboard ordnance station of this AH-1F's stub wing. These braces help steady the ejector rack fitted to the wing pylon, preventing ordnance from excessive swaying while in flight. A mooring ring is fitted to the forward wing root; a second ring is placed farther aft on the stub wing. (Author)

Towing rings are fitted to the nose of each Cobra landing skid. Shoes bolted to the skid undersurfaces protect the skids from excessive wear from hard landing surfaces. A four-tube TOW launcher and a seven-tube rocket pod are fitted to the right stub wing of this AH-1. (Author)

Three access panels are flush fitted to the port tail boom on AH-1S series helicopters. These panels allow access to armament system control components and the tail rotor linkage. An Ultra High Frequency (UHF) radio antenna is fitted to the boom undersurface. (Author)

The blade antenna on the undersurface of this AH-1F's tail boom is for the Cobra's Very High Frequency (VHF) radio. A UHF 'hockey stick' antenna is placed aft of the VHF antenna. The small blade antenna further aft is for the AH-1F's Identification Friend or Foe (IFF) transponder, which sends a coded radio signal to ground stations and other aircraft. A tail skid is mounted on the tail boom's aft end. (Author)

A tail skid – commonly called the stinger – is standard on all Cobras. It protects the tail rotor during tail-low landings. A streamlined fairing protects the tail rotor gearbox, which is located opposite the rotor hub. The circular areas on the tail boom indicate the location for a handle-shaped VHF Omnidirectional Radio (VOR) navigation system antenna. (Author)

Tail booms of Cobra models from the AH-1Q and AH-1J are equipped with a synchronized, single-piece elevator. It spans 6 feet, 11 inches (2.1 M) and mechanically moves up or down to enhance stability and trim. The 1st Cavalry Division's insignia is painted under the serial number (0-15813) on the tail fin. (Author)

A late AH-1F modification is the Tracor M-130 30-cartridge chaff/flare dispenser fitted to the aft tail boom. Chaff – aluminum-covered plastic film – counters radar-guided missiles, while flares decoy IR-guided missiles. A fairing immediately forward of the M-130 houses an NVG position light (top) and a clear navigation light. (David Roof)

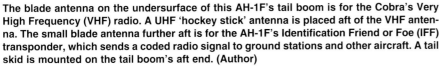

This Sand (FS33717) Modernized AH-1S Cobra (66-15339) was originally an early model AH-1G. Thick canopy framing identifies its earlier flat plate canopy. It has not been equipped with air inlet diverters or the IR jammer atop the exhaust section. The box unusually fitted under the laser tracker on the rotor pylon housed the tracker's components. These components were later relocated inside the pylon. (Terry Love)

The TAH-1F is the trainer version of the AH-1F Modernized Cobra. All weapons are removed and ballast is placed inside the turret. Nose and fuselage panels and the elevators are International Orange (FS12197) on the overall Helo Drab (FS34031) aircraft. This TAH-1F, White 55, is parked at an Army airfield in October of 1983. (Ted Paskowski via Terry Love)

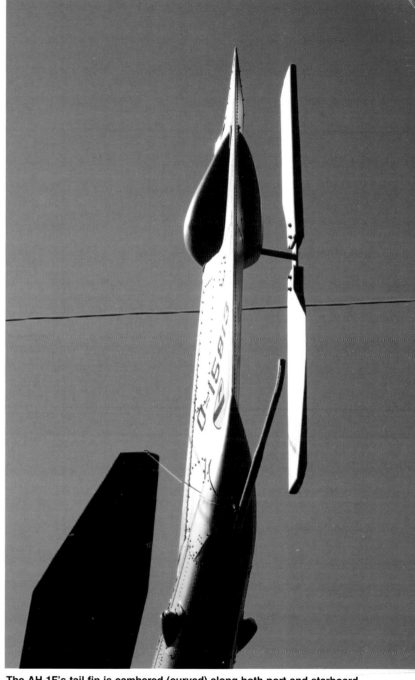

The AH-1F's tail fin is cambered (curved) along both port and starboard sides. This camber offsets the torque-induced yaw (rotation about the vertical axis) from the main rotor. The tail rotor gearbox and hub are placed within a teardrop-shaped fairing on the upper tail fin surface. A tail skid is mounted on the tail boom end. (Author)

(Above) This AH-1F (79-23241) of the 268th Attack Helicopter Battery at Fort Lewis, Washington is displayed at Coast Guard Air Station (CGAS) Port Angeles, Washington in April of 1986. The helicopter is overall Helo Drab, which is worn along the edges of removable access panels. Canopy edges are white, which is unusual for a front line Cobra. The aircraft is armed with a 20mm M197 cannon in a Universal Turret System (UTS). A 19-tube M200 rocket pod is mounted on the inboard port wing station, while a four-tube TOW launcher – with one BGM-71 TOW missile loaded – is placed on the outboard station. A cable secures the main rotor blade tip to the tail boom, preventing the rotor from freely rotating in the wind. (Don Abrahamson via Terry Love)

(Left) This AH-1F of the 18th Cavalry Regiment, California National Guard is parked at its home base of Los Alamitos, California. It is armed with M261 rocket pods and two-cell TOW launchers. The National Guard insignia is placed on the aft rotor pylon section. An orange cover is fitted over the IR-suppressing exhaust nozzle. The last three digits of the AH-1F's serial number (073) are white, which is frequent in Guard units for easy identification of aircraft. (Skip Robinson)

The AH-1T Improved SeaCobra – like its predecessor, the AH-1J SeaCobra – was larger than single-engine Cobras. The AH-1T's fuselage length of 45 feet 6 inches (13.9 M) was one foot (0.3 M) longer than the AH-1J. This new variant was equipped for the TOW anti-tank missile system. This aircraft also received an uprated 1970 SHP Pratt & Whitney Canada T400-WV-402 coupled turboshaft engine, a ventral fin, and a redesigned tail fin. The first 'Tango' Cobra (BuNo 159228), modified from an AH-1J, skims the tree tops on an evaluation flight in 1976. The AH-1T evolved into the AH-1W (originally AH-1T+), the first of which was delivered to the Marines in 1986. (Bell)

A Marine AH-1W 'Whiskey' Cobra rests at a Coalition airbase during Operation DESERT STORM – the 1991 Persian Gulf War against Iraq. The 20mm M197 cannon is mounted in a universal turret under the nose. Unlike Army Cobras, turrets on Marine AH-1s have coverings placed around the drive assembly to prevent corrosion from sea spray. The AH-1W is armed with a LAU-68 rocket pod under the stub wing inboard station. Each LAU-68 holds seven 2.75 inch (70mm) WAFARs. A 19-tube LAU-61 pod with M257 illumination rockets is placed under the outboard wing station. This 'Whiskey' is camouflaged in Sand (FS33711) and Brown (FS30117) for Persian Gulf operations. (Bell)

An AH-1W (BuNo 162547) makes a low altitude flight over the southwest United States. It is assigned to Marine Helicopter Attack Squadron, Light (HMLA)-169 'Vipers,' based at Marine Corps Air Facility (MCAF) Camp Pendleton, California. The 'Whiskey' Cobra is armed with Motorola AGM-122 Sidearm short-range, anti-radiation missiles on the outer wing stations. The Sidearm is a converted AIM-9C Sidewinder air-to-air missile intended for low-altitude use against air defense weapons. This SeaCobra is camouflaged in Blue Gray (FS35237), Flat Black (FS37038), and Field Green (FS34095). (Bell)

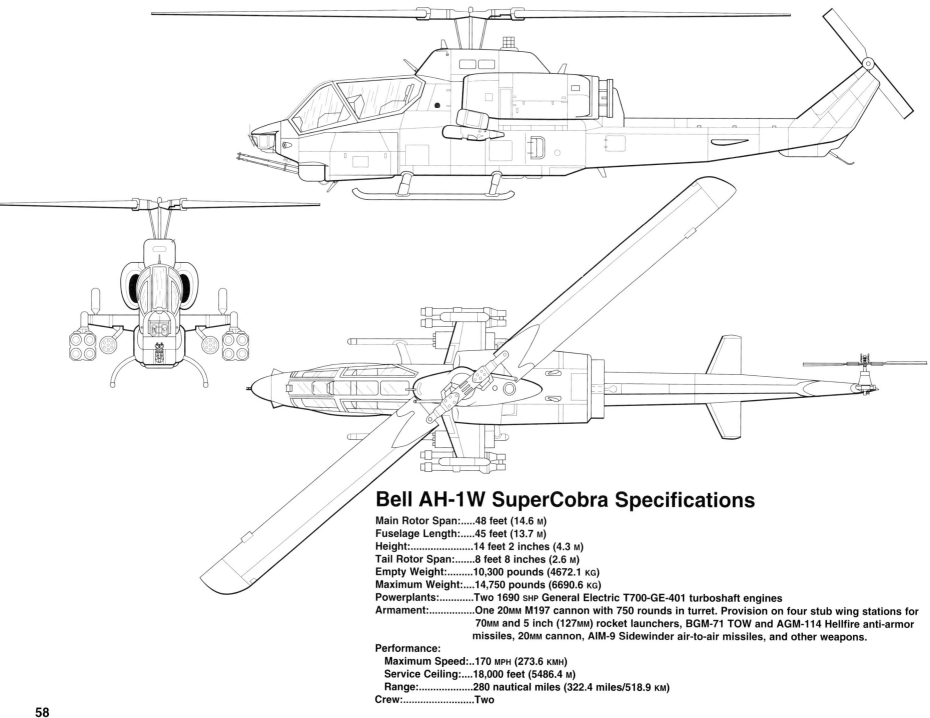

Bell AH-1W SuperCobra Specifications

Main Rotor Span:.....48 feet (14.6 M)
Fuselage Length:.....45 feet (13.7 M)
Height:......................14 feet 2 inches (4.3 M)
Tail Rotor Span:.......8 feet 8 inches (2.6 M)
Empty Weight:.........10,300 pounds (4672.1 KG)
Maximum Weight:....14,750 pounds (6690.6 KG)
Powerplants:............Two 1690 SHP General Electric T700-GE-401 turboshaft engines
Armament:................One 20MM M197 cannon with 750 rounds in turret. Provision on four stub wing stations for
70MM and 5 inch (127MM) rocket launchers, BGM-71 TOW and AGM-114 Hellfire anti-armor
missiles, 20MM cannon, AIM-9 Sidewinder air-to-air missiles, and other weapons.

Performance:
   Maximum Speed:..170 MPH (273.6 KMH)
    Service Ceiling:....18,000 feet (5486.4 M)
     Range:...................280 nautical miles (322.4 miles/518.9 KM)
Crew:.........................Two

A Marine AH-1W 'Whiskey' Cobra makes a low-altitude pass. It is armed with 38 2.75-inch Hydra rockets in two 19-tube pods on the inboard stub wing stations. A four-tube BGM-71 TOW launcher is mounted on the starboard outer wing station, while Rockwell AGM-114 Hellfire missiles are mounted on the port wing. The SuperCobra is the only helicopter in the world capable of launching both TOW and Hellfire anti-armor missiles. AH-1Ws were deployed to Afghanistan in November of 2001 to hunt down and destroy al-Qaeda terrorist forces. These terrorists are believed responsible for the 11 September 2001 attacks on New York's World Trade Center and the Pentagon in Washington. (Bell)

Rockwell AGM-114 Hellfire (HELicopter Launched FIRE-and-forget) Missile

Hydra 70 2.75 Inch (70mm) Rocket Pods

Seven-Tube Pod

19-Tube Pod

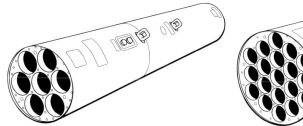

(Right) Triangular-shaped vents are added to the underside of the AH-1W's nose extension. These vents help cool components of the nose-mounted M65 Telescopic Sight Unit (TSU). The gunner/copilot in the front cockpit uses the TSU to track targets and aim weapons at those targets. The port forward antenna for the American Electronic Laboratories (AEL) AN/APR-44 radar warning system is placed in a fairing aft of the TSU turret. (David Roof)

The TOW sighting unit dominates the AH-1W gunner/copilot's cockpit. The armament control display is placed to port of the TOW sight. A standby compass is attached to the left forward canopy frame. The gray cylindrical throttle/collective lever is placed on the port cockpit side, while the cyclic stick is located to starboard. (David Roof)

The AH-1W pilot's cockpit differs in only minor details from the cockpit of the earlier AH-1J. The artificial horizon is placed at the upper center panel section, with other flight instruments located nearby. Paired engine gauges are placed in a light gray panel on the lower left instrument panel. The cyclic stick is mounted between the pilot's legs. (David Roof)

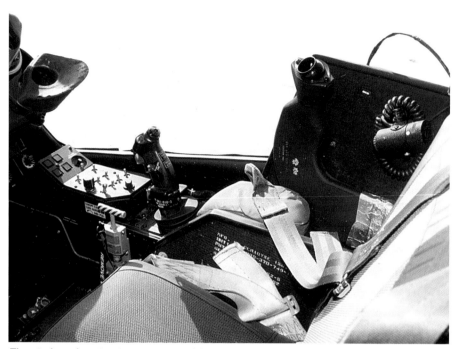

The starboard seat outer armor panel in the gunner/copilot's cockpit incorporates a circular ventilation duct and a Grimes map light on a coiled cord. Between the inner and outer armor panels is an armrest for operating the cyclic control. The yellow and black striped T-shaped handle beside the cyclic grip is the canopy emergency release handle. (David Roof)

The Heads Up Display (HUD) unit is mounted above the AH-1W's instrument panel. The radar warning scope is placed to starboard of the HUD, while the AN/ALE-39 chaff/flare control unit is located to the warning scope's right. Links to the Helmet Sight Subsystem (HSS) are mounted along the upper canopy rail. (David Roof)

The large lever along the AH-1W's pilot station is the rotor brake, which stops the main rotor's rotation. The Marines specified rotor brakes on their Cobras, due to their safety benefits while operating from ships. The launcher arming switch is located below the rotor brake lever. The emergency canopy release handle is placed within the indentation in the center of the pilot's seat. (David Roof)

Electronic equipment is mounted on the aft cockpit bulkhead, behind the pilot's seat. Small armor panels are placed atop the seat back, while larger panels are fitted to the sides of the seat. The seat temperature control hose mounted on the bulkhead supplies cooled or heated air to the pilot from the environmental control system. (David Roof)

The pilot's collective control lever is mounted on the port cockpit console. The circular throttle grip is mounted high on the collective lever. A bulky unit housing various controls is placed atop the lever. Among the controls located here are the engine start switch and stores release controls. AH-1W cockpit components are mainly painted Instrument Black (FS27038) and Flat Black (FS37038). (David Roof)

(Above) The access panel for the hydraulic reservoir and rotor brake master cylinder is placed between the aft cockpit and the engine air intake on the AH-1W. This panel is marked with a jet intake warning found on all Navy and Marine aircraft. The AH-1W makes liberal use of small access panels, compared to previous SeaCobra variants. These panels increase ease of access to various components, which helps improve servicing. The flush hinged step near the intake's leading edge extends out and downward for crew use during maintenance and inspection. A protective cover is placed over the AN/ALE-39 chaff/flare dispenser mounted atop the stub wing. (David Roof)

Engines Used by AH-1 Variants

AH-1G/Q	One 1400 SHP Avco Lycoming T53-L-13 engine
AH-1S/P/F	One 1800 SHP Avco Lycoming T53-L-703 engine
AH-1J	One 1800 SHP Pratt & Whitney Canada PT6T-4 'Twin Pac' coupled engine
AH-1T	One 1970 SHP Pratt & Whitney Canada T400-WV-402 'Twin Pac' coupled engine
AH-1W	Two 1690 SHP General Electric T700-GE-401 engines

(Left) Although the AH-1W retains the slim profile of its predecessors, the cockpit has become more crowded as systems were added and improved. The canopy for the gunner/copilot opens to port, while the pilot's access is to starboard; this is the same as for other Cobra variants. The armchair collective/throttle – lacking the usual control housing box – is mounted on the port console, beside the canopy rail. A red fire extinguisher is tucked behind the seat, while hand holds and helmet sight links are attached to the upper canopy frames. Crew seats on Marine Cobras are Dark Gull Gray (FS36231) trimmed in Olive Drab (FS34087), with Interior Green (FS34151) seat belts. (David Roof)

(Above) A combined AN/APX-100(V) Identification Friend or Foe (IFF) and AN/ARC-182(V) Frequency Modulation (FM) radio antenna is located on the AH-1W's rotor pylon, just forward of the rotor mast. Another such antenna is placed on the fuselage undersurface. The bulge just aft of the pitot tube is formed into both sides of the rotor pylon to provide room for rotor components. (David Roof)

(Above Right) The rotor mast supports the AH-1W's all-black rotor head, with pitch controlled by two tubes at each side and attached to pitch horns. Input from the pilot's collective stick alters the rotor pitch, while the cyclic stick input tilts the rotor disc in the desired direction. Both rotor blades are attached to the rotor head through grips and a large pin. Drag braces connected to the blades' trailing edge resist drag forces upon the rotor blades. The AH-1W's all-metal main rotor blades are 48 feet (14.6 M) in diameter, with a 33-inch (83.8 CM) chord (width). The rotor blades have swept tips to reduce noise and improve high speed performance. (David Roof)

(Right) The 'Whiskey' Cobra's engine access doors provide ample space for maintenance. The opened lower door provides a sturdy work platform for ground crews. Easy maintenance access is greatly appreciated by Marine crews operating in the field. Black non-skid material is applied to the stub wing walkway area on this desert camouflaged Cobra.

An AH-1W SuperCobra is assembled at Bell Helicopter's Fort Worth, Texas plant. The engine compartment access doors are open, revealing the starboard 1690 SHP General Electric T700-GE-401 turboshaft engine. A red anti-Foreign Object Damage (FOD) cover is placed over the engine exhaust to prevent objects being dropped inside during construc- tion. Other access panels on the center and forward fuselage have not been installed on this SuperCobra. These panels include those for the transmission compartment, located immediately forward of the engines. Most metal surfaces are primed in Lusterless Green (FS34516). (Bell)

This AH-1W (WR-721/BuNo 164576) is assigned to HMLA-775 'Coyotes,' a Marine Corps Reserve unit at MCAF Camp Pendleton. The SuperCobra is armed with Ford Aerospace AIM-9 Sidewinder air-to-air missiles on its outboard ejector racks. Later model AH-1Ws have slightly shorter and bulkier canopies to accommodate the Night Targeting Systems (NTS) added to the nose area. This SuperCobra is painted Blue Gray (FS35237) and Light Ghost Gray (FS36375). (David Roof)

A Hellfire Missile Launcher (HML) is mounted under the starboard wing of an AH-1W. This launcher carries four Rockwell AGM-114 Hellfire (HELicopter Launched FIRE and forget) anti-tank missiles. Electrical firing cables run through tubing at the front of the forward support connecting the top and bottom rails. An empty ejector rack is mounted on the inboard wing station. The two small bulges on the wingtip are a position light (green) and a Night Vision Goggle (NVG) position light (white) (David Roof)

Four AGM-114 Hellfires are loaded onto an HML mounted under the starboard wing of an HMLA-167 AH-1W. Yellow protective caps cover the glass nose while the aircraft is on the ground. A laser seeker in the nose guides Hellfire to its designated target. The AGM-114 has a range of 4.3 nautical miles (4.95 miles/7.97 км). A laser seeker in its glass nose broadens its search capability. Hellfires fired from Marine AH-1Ws during DESERT STORM were successful against armor and hard targets, with similar results occurring more recently in Afghanistan. (US Army)

A 100 gallon (378.5 L) external fuel tank is mounted on this AH-1W's inboard wing rack, while an AIM-9 Sidewinder air-to-air missile is placed on the outboard rack. The SuperCobra is cleared to carry either 100 gallon or 78 gallon (295.3 L) capacity fuel tanks for increased range. Other stores carried on the inboard racks include rocket and cannon pods, and Fuel-Air Explosive (FAE) bombs. Marine policy dictates that AIM-9s be transported to the aircraft without fins, which are later installed on the missiles. (David Roof)

A two-tube BGM-71 TOW (Tube-launched, Optically-tracked, Wire-guided) anti-tank missile launcher is mounted on the port outboard wing pylon of this AH-1W. An external fuel tank is loaded onto the inboard wing pylon. A black electrical cable runs down the inboard side of the AN/ALE-39 chaff/flare dispenser. (David Roof)

The Tracor AN/ALE-39 chaff/flare dispenser is standard equipment on the AH-1W. The 30-cartridge dispenser is mounted on the stub wings. A combination of chaff cartridges for decoying radar-homing missiles and flares to decoy heat-seeking missiles is carried in the AN/ALE-39. These cartridges are launched either manually by the pilot or gunner/copilot, or automatically using preset programs set into the dispenser system. No cartridges are fitted into this AN/ALE dispenser. (US Marine Corps)

Crew access steps are attached to the AH-1W's fuselage, forward and aft of the stub wing. Three mooring rings located at each wing root help secure the SuperCobra to the ship's deck. Cables attach the rings to mooring spots on the flight deck. A seven-tube 2.75 inch LAU-68/A rocket pod is mounted on the inboard wing pylon. (David Roof)

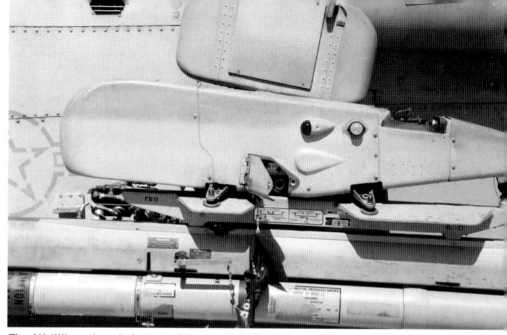

The AH-1W's outboard wing station – called an ejector rack in Marine aviation – can accommodate launchers for AIM-9, TOW, or Hellfire missiles. A two-cell TOW launcher is attached to the port outboard ejector rack of this SuperCobra. A seven-tube 2.75 inch LAU-68/A rocket pod is secured to the inboard ejector rack. (David Roof)

The AH-1W's outboard ejector rack is streamlined to match the wing's airfoil. An open panel on the wingtip provides access for the ejector rack connection to the wingtip. The ADU-299 pylon adapter is fitted to the ejector rack to enable an LAU-7 missile launcher to be installed. An AIM-9 Sidewinder air-to-air missile is attached to the LAU-7 launcher. (David Roof)

An ADU-299 pylon adapter was fitted to the AH-1W's outboard ejector rack before the LAU-7 launcher was installed. This launcher is used to fire AIM-9 Sidewinders, which the SuperCobras use for self-defense against enemy fixed-wing aircraft and helicopters. An LAU-68/A rocket launcher occupies the sturdy inboard rack. (David Roof)

The ADU-299 pylon adapter is fitted to the outboard ejection rack using fore-and-aft lugs. Two pairs of sway braces attach to the adapter, preventing it from swaying in the air. The SuperCobra's stub wings span 11 feet 7 inches (3.5 M), compared to the 10 feet 9 inch (3.3 M) span of earlier AH-1S/F Cobras. (David Roof)

This AH-1W (WR-721/BuNo 164576) of HMLA-775 'Coyotes' is displayed at Naval Air Station (NAS) Miramar, California in 1996. The Marine Reserve Squadron is based as MCAF Camp Pendleton. A Sanders AN/ALQ-144 pulsed Infrared (IR) jammer is mounted atop the rotor pylon , aft of the main rotor mast. This device sends heat pulses away from the aircraft to decoy IR-homing missiles. Threat warning receivers project from both sides of the rotor pylon. Two AN/ARC-114A FM homing blade antennas are mounted atop the engine nacelles. The blunted trailing edge of the cambered tail fin reduces torque-induced yaw. (David Roof)

AN/ALQ-144 Pulsed Infrared Jammer

AH-1W Cobras updated with the Night Targeting System (NTS) are equipped with light yellow flush formation light strips. These electroluminescent lights are applied to the tail fin, lower forward tail boom, and the forward fuselage below the canopy. The brightness of these lights is adjustable to match night and low visibility flying conditions. An avionics bay access hatch is fitted above and aft of the light strip. The black ventral combination antenna for the AN/APX-100(V) IFF system and AN/ARC-182(V) FM radio is mounted on the fuselage undersurface. The ventral fairing forward of the antenna is a transmission blower exhaust outlet. (David Roof)

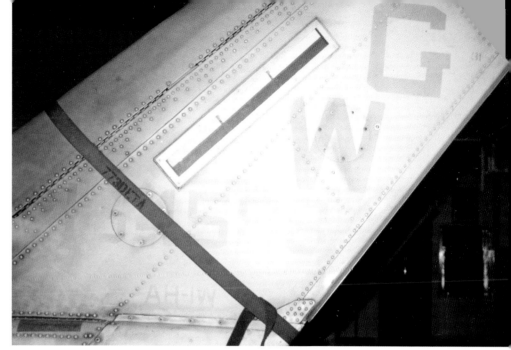

The transmission blower exhaust fairing is mounted on the fuselage undersurface, aft of the landing skids. This vents heated air from the AH-1W's engine transmission system. A hydraulic motor driven fan supplies cooling air to both heat exchangers servicing the transmission and gearbox oil cooler. (David Roof)

The black portion of the light yellow formation light strips used in conjunction with the NTS emits an IR signal. This portion is only visible to wearers of Night Vision Goggles (NVGs). The 'WG' tail code of this AH-1W (BuNo 164588) denotes HMLA-775, Detachment A at Johnstown, Pennsylvania. The Reserve Squadron's home base is NAS Willow Grove, Pennsylvania. (David Roof)

The AH-1W's tail rotor gearbox, hub, and rotor blade grips protrude from the upper starboard tail fin section. Pitch links are extended through the top of the cambered tail fin. A cylindrical oil filler and cap are mounted atop the gearbox. (David Roof)

The SuperCobra's tail rotor system is Flat Black (FS37038) – the same color used for the main rotor components and blades. A screened vent was added to the top portion of the tail fin. The flat plate atop the 90˚ gearbox is a Global Positioning System (GPS) antenna, which gathers precise navigation data from satellites. (David Roof)

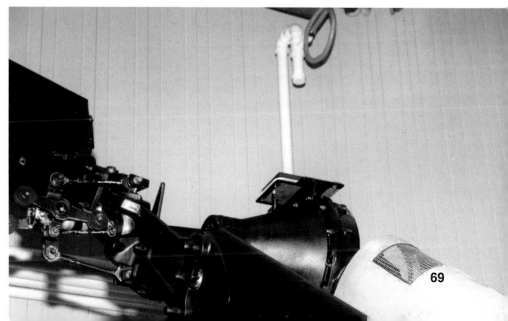

An AH-1W SuperCobra banks to port while it flies low over the China Lake Naval Air Warfare Center (NAWC), California in 1991. The aircraft is assigned to Air Test and Evaluation Squadron 1 (VX-1) 'Pioneers,' based at China Lake. VX-1 flies the AH-1W and other Navy and Marine aircraft on test and evaluation duties. The SuperCobra's stub wings are clean (without stores) for this test flight. This AH-1W is finished in the Tactical Paint Scheme (TPS) of Field Green (FS34095), Flat Black (FS37038), and Blue Gray (FS35237). (Vance Vasquez/NAWCWPNS)

70

Four AH-1Ws assigned to HMLA-264 prepare to depart from USS WASP (LHD-1) during Joint Task Force Exercise 98-1 in the Atlantic on 13 January 1998. The aft SuperCobra has entered a 'hover taxi' above the flight deck, awaiting the takeoff of the other three helicopters. This exercise tested the ability of joint forces to rapidly deploy and conduct joint operations during a crisis. HMLA-264 — formerly HMM-264, a medium transport unit – is based at MCAS New River, North Carolina. (DOD by PO3C Kenneth L. Pace, USN)

Two AH-1Ws fly over the live fire range at Glamoc, Bosnia and Herzegovina on 2 April 1998. Rocket pods are fitted to the inboard stub wing pylons, while a TOW missile launcher is mounted on the port outboard pylon. These helicopters are participating in Exercise DYNAMIC RESPONSE 98, which is designed to familiarize reserve forces with the territory and their operational capabilities within this region. The SuperCobras are assigned to the 26th Marine Expeditionary Unit (MEU), which serves as the Strategic Reserve Force of the multi-national Stabilization Force (SFOR) in Bosnia and Herzegovina. SFOR maintains the peace among the Muslim, Croat, and Serb peoples in this former province of Yugoslavia. The aircraft assigned to the Force have SFOR painted on the airframe; these AH-1Ws have the title painted on the engine nacelles. (DOD by CPO Steve Briggs, USN)

71

This AH-1G Cobra (69-16440) was assigned to the 120th Aviation Company 'Arctic Knights' at Fort Richardson, Alaska during the late 1960s and into the 1970s. It is finished in the arctic high visibility scheme of Gloss White (FS17875) and Insignia Red (FS11136). The last three digits of the serial number are painted on the front of the rotor pylon.

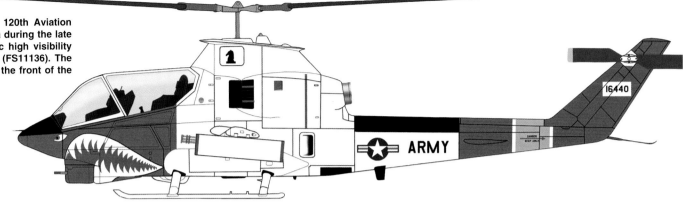

Pandora's Box was an AH-1G (68-17031) that served in the latter part of the Vietnam War. It is armed with the 20MM XM-35 cannon on the inboard wing station, with ammunition stored in streamlined fairings attached to both sides of the lower fuselage. An XM-158 rocket launcher was usually carried on the outboard rack, with rocket pods also on the opposite wing. The AH-1G's overall Olive Drab (FS34087) finish was retouched on parts of the airframe.

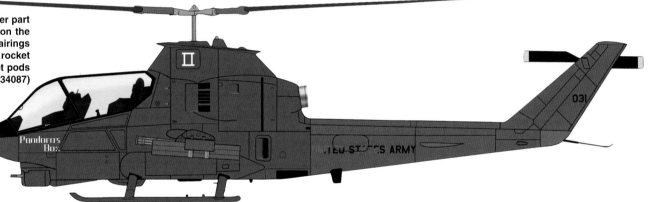

This AH-1G (67-15687) was assigned to the 7th Squadron, 1st Cavalry Regiment in Vietnam. Cobras were naturals for the famed shark mouth, with at least 12 different styles painted on Army and Marine AH-1Gs in Vietnam. Two XM-158 and two XM-200 rocket launchers are mounted on the wings. The Regiment and Squadron designation is painted under the Cobra's nose. A replacement tail rotor blade with yellow trim was installed on this aircraft.

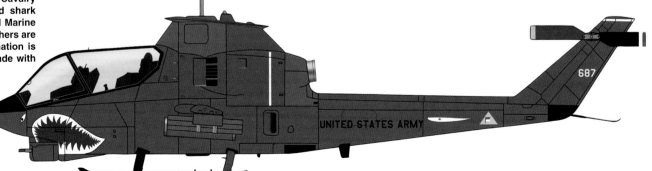

The US Navy Test Pilot's School (TPS) at Naval Air Station (NAS) Patuxent River, Maryland borrowed this AH-1G (52/68-15045) from Marine Attack Helicopter Squadron 773 (HMA-773). The school used the Cobra to further evaluate the type during the post-Vietnam War years. The TPS added only its tail fin band to complement HMA-773's colorful markings. The AH-1G was overall glossy Field Green (FS14097), with an Orange Yellow (FS13538) tail boom band.

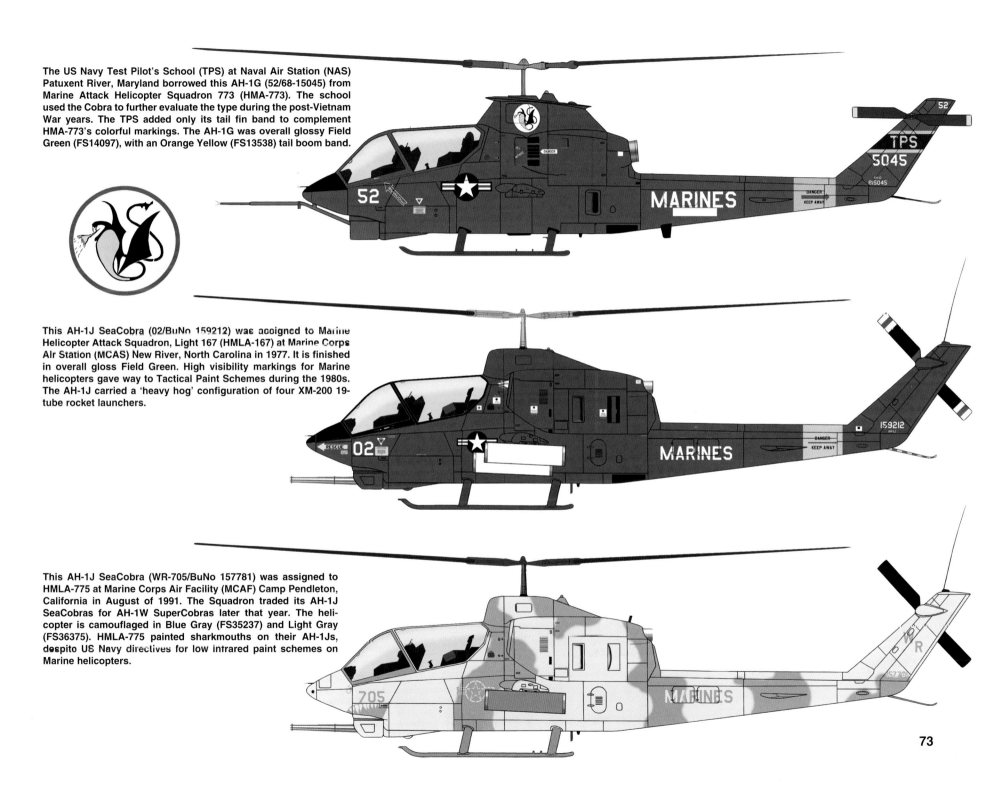

This AH-1J SeaCobra (02/BuNo 159212) was assigned to Marine Helicopter Attack Squadron, Light 167 (HMLA-167) at Marine Corps Air Station (MCAS) New River, North Carolina in 1977. It is finished in overall gloss Field Green. High visibility markings for Marine helicopters gave way to Tactical Paint Schemes during the 1980s. The AH-1J carried a 'heavy hog' configuration of four XM-200 19-tube rocket launchers.

This AH-1J SeaCobra (WR-705/BuNo 157781) was assigned to HMLA-775 at Marine Corps Air Facility (MCAF) Camp Pendleton, California in August of 1991. The Squadron traded its AH-1J SeaCobras for AH-1W SuperCobras later that year. The helicopter is camouflaged in Blue Gray (FS35237) and Light Gray (FS36375). HMLA-775 painted sharkmouths on their AH-1Js, despite US Navy directives for low intrared paint schemes on Marine helicopters.

(Above) This AH-1W (BuNo 161022) was converted to an AH-1(4B)W (Four-Bladed 'Whiskey') in 1989. This SuperCobra serves as the test bed for the Cobra the US Marines will take to the year 2025—the AH-1Z. The 'H-1 Upgrade' involves the remanufacture of AH-1Ws in conjunction with Marine Bell UH-1N 'Twin Huey' transport helicopters. Eighty-five percent of maintenance significant components are identical to both aircraft types. Obvious differences in the AH-1(4B)W from the AH-1W are the Bell Advanced 680 four-bladed rotor system with composite blades and elevator end fins. The aircraft is overall Field Green with black markings; however, the 19-tube LAU-69 rocket pod under the port outer wing station is white. (Bell)

(Left) The first AH-1Z Cobra (BuNo 162549) makes its maiden flight from Bell's Arlington, Texas airfield on 7 December 2000. The 'Zulu' is fitted with a four-bladed main and tail rotors. The near bearingless rotor system doubles its payload capacity over the earlier AH-1W and dramatically increases the SuperCobra's flight envelope. Other outward changes are a redesigned nose, revamped stub wing ejectors, elevator tail fins, and an enlarged rotor pylon. The latter accommodates a Sunstrand Auxiliary Power Unit (APU), which drives an Alternating Current (AC) generator. Three AH-1Zs, along with three UH-1Ys (UH-1Ns with four-bladed rotors), are scheduled for testing into 2003. (Bell)

The prototype AH-1(4B)W gunner/copilot's instrument panel is a refined version of the panel selected for the AH-1Z. Analog flight instruments used on previous Cobra variants are replaced by two Multi-Purpose Displays (MPDs). The port MPD presents weapon information, while the color MPD to starboard displays flight data. The combined collective lever and throttle are placed on the port console, while the cyclic stick is located on the starboard console. This digitally integrated gunner/copilot's cockpit is similar to the pilot's station in the AH-1Z. (Bell)

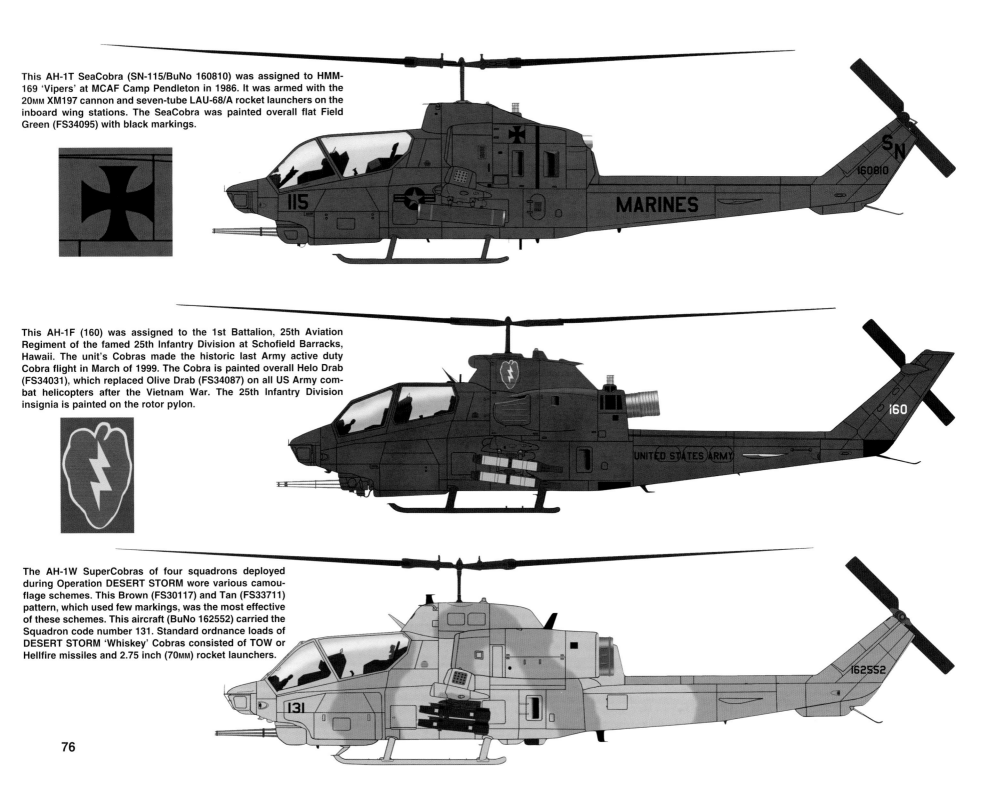

This AH-1T SeaCobra (SN-115/BuNo 160810) was assigned to HMM-169 'Vipers' at MCAF Camp Pendleton in 1986. It was armed with the 20MM XM197 cannon and seven-tube LAU-68/A rocket launchers on the inboard wing stations. The SeaCobra was painted overall flat Field Green (FS34095) with black markings.

This AH-1F (160) was assigned to the 1st Battalion, 25th Aviation Regiment of the famed 25th Infantry Division at Schofield Barracks, Hawaii. The unit's Cobras made the historic last Army active duty Cobra flight in March of 1999. The Cobra is painted overall Helo Drab (FS34031), which replaced Olive Drab (FS34087) on all US Army combat helicopters after the Vietnam War. The 25th Infantry Division insignia is painted on the rotor pylon.

The AH-1W SuperCobras of four squadrons deployed during Operation DESERT STORM wore various camouflage schemes. This Brown (FS30117) and Tan (FS33711) pattern, which used few markings, was the most effective of these schemes. This aircraft (BuNo 162552) carried the Squadron code number 131. Standard ordnance loads of DESERT STORM 'Whiskey' Cobras consisted of TOW or Hellfire missiles and 2.75 inch (70MM) rocket launchers.

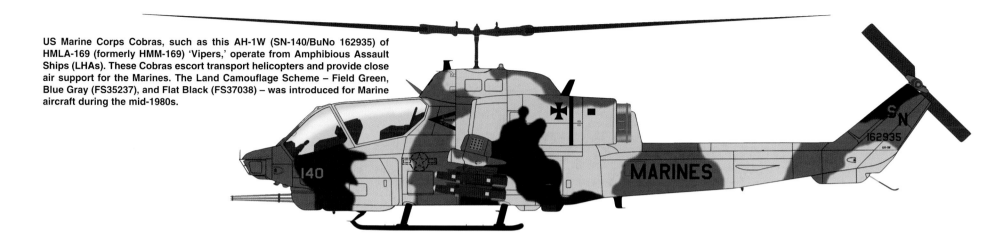

US Marine Corps Cobras, such as this AH-1W (SN-140/BuNo 162935) of HMLA-169 (formerly HMM-169) 'Vipers,' operate from Amphibious Assault Ships (LHAs). These Cobras escort transport helicopters and provide close air support for the Marines. The Land Camouflage Scheme – Field Green, Blue Gray (FS35237), and Flat Black (FS37038) – was introduced for Marine aircraft during the mid-1980s.

This AH-1W (ES-30/BuNo 160816) of HMM-266 'Griffins' is equipped with the Night Targeting System (NTS), which is identified by light yellow night vision strips on the tail fin, tail boom, and forward fuselage. Camouflage colors are Blue Gray over Light Gray (FS36375). The Squadron is based at MCAS New River, North Carolina.

The ultra modern AH-1Z is finished in the Blue Gray over Light Gray camouflage scheme familiar to the AH-1W; however, its design differs dramatically from the 'Whiskey' Cobra. Built from existing AH-1Ws, the AH-1Z is the next generation Cobra. This AH-1Z (BuNo 162549) is the first of two 'Zulu' Cobras built and assigned to NAS Patuxent River, Maryland for evaluation trials.

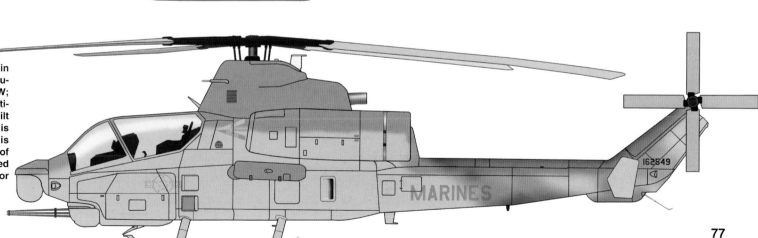

77

The AH-1Z features a nose-mounted Hawkeye Target Sighting System (TSS), which is integrated with the Cobra Radar System. This system automatically searches, detects, classifies, and prioritizes multiple moving and stationary targets on land and in the air in low-visible conditions. Fitting the TSS in the AH-1Z's nose results in a shorter gunner/copilot canopy. (US Navy)

Two General Electric T700 series turboshaft engines power the AH-1Z, similar to the 1690 SHP T700-GE-401 used by the AH-1W. T700 series powerplants also power the Army's two main helicopters, the Boeing AH-64 Apache and the Sikorsky UH-60 Black Hawk. (US Navy)

The outboard ejector racks differ in size and shape from those fitted to the earlier AH-1W. These new racks allow installation of AIM-9 Sidewinder launchers to the outboard pylon face. The AH-1Z's four universal wing store stations can carry any combination of rocket pods, M299 Hellfire launchers, TOW launchers, and external fuel tanks. (US Navy)

The AH-1Z is equipped with a Hover Infrared Suppression System (HISS), similar to that used by the earlier AH-1W. The HISS uses engine compartment and outside air for cooling; however, the AH-1Z's system adds an outer panel for additional cooling. The APU exhaust port is placed at the aft section of the rotor pylon. It starts the engine on battery power alone in temperatures well below freezing. (US Navy)

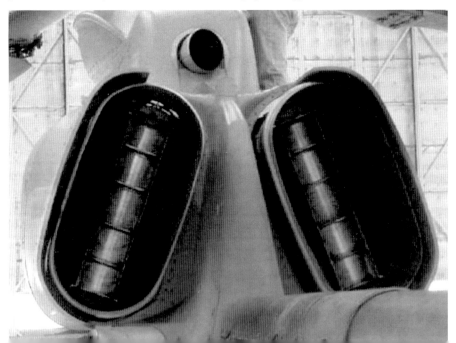

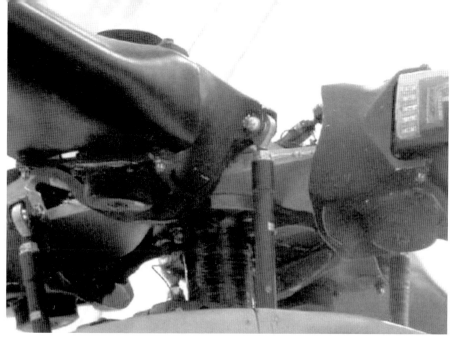

Few items of the AH-1Z main rotor controls extend beyond the rotor pylon, unlike in previous Cobra variants. The new variant's high performance lies in its main rotor system, which eliminates all bearings, hinges, and dampers. Its primary components are two stacked fiberglass yokes, each supporting two fiberglass/epoxy composite blades. (US Navy)

The AH-1Z's tail rotor consists of two stacked rotors, which are independently mounted on a single shaft. The rotor is returned to the port 'pusher' side of the aircraft, where it was installed on the early AH-1Gs. Most Cobras had the tail rotor mounted on the starboard 'tractor' side for additional flight stability. (US Navy)

The AH-1Z's elevators are equipped with additional end fins to aid in directional stability. The fins are fixed to the elevator ends and move up or down with the elevators as required. More directional stability is conferred by the ventral tail boom fairing, which is carried over from the AH-1W. A tail skid is fitted to the ventral fairing. (US Navy)

An elaborate, yet simplistic tail rotor system is installed on the AH-1Z. It features one pair of rotor blades stacked over another pair, with the pitch control links connected to the hub. The four-bladed main rotor uses this same arrangement. Four-bladed rotors produce less vibration and noise than two-bladed rotors. (US Navy)

Detail & Scale Books

8241 F-89 Scorpion

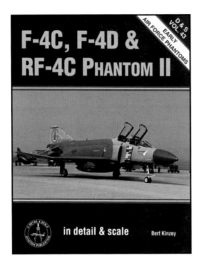

8243 F-4C/D, RF-4C Phantom II

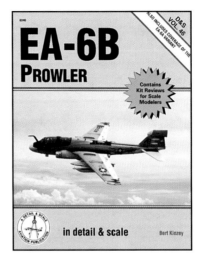

8246 EA-6B Prowler

8247 B-36 Peacemaker

8256 F4U Corsair, Part 2

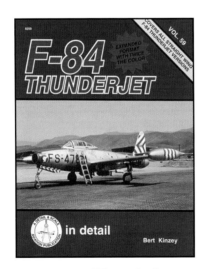

8259 F-84 Thunderjet

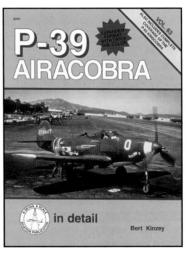

8263 P-39 Airacobra

8264 B-24 Liberator

from squadron/signal publications